Making Soup in a Storm

(NEW WRITING SCOTLAND 24)

Edited by

Valerie Thornton

and

Brian Whittingham

Association for Scottish Literary Studies

Association for Scottish Literary Studies
c/o Department of Scottish History, 9 University Gardens
University of Glasgow, Glasgow G12 8QH
www.asls.org.uk

First published 2006

British Library Cataloguing in Publication Data

A CIP record for this book is available
from the British Library

ISBN: 0-948877-72-3
ISBN-13: 978-0-948877-72-8

The Association for Scottish Literary Studies
acknowledges the support of the Scottish Arts Council
towards the publication of this book

Typeset by AFS Image Setters Ltd, Glasgow

Printed by Bell & Bain Ltd, Glasgow

CONTENTS

INTRODUCTION

Soup requires ingredients and gives one a feeling of internal warmth. A storm results in movement that is remembered by any who experience it. As editors of *New Writing Scotland* 24, we were on the lookout for fresh linguistic ingredients that moved our emotions, engaged our intellect, and warmed us inside, believing that this is what the reader needs to have their attention captured and sustained. We hope the pieces we have selected will move you and be memorable.

The quest to fit submissions into the required criteria was both arduous and rewarding. Why arduous? Let's look at statistics. Out of over 1,150 submissions (830 poems, 320 short stories and 3 playscripts), each of us found fewer than 30 pieces of work, that, for us, hit the spot. Some pieces one editor favoured, other pieces the other editor favoured, some pieces we both found inspiring as is the nature of the process. So, roughly a 4 per cent acceptance rate of what we perceived to be the most successful writing.

For us this work stood out because it was well structured, well edited (in terms of punctuation, spelling and layout – yes, there are still a number of submissions that are lazily crafted and shoddily produced), had an original viewpoint, was capable of a precision of expression, had emotional sincerity and intellectual integrity.

The result was a total of 43 pieces being accepted, and that's where the rewarding part came into it. To read work that engages and grabs your soul is indeed a pleasure. Work with strong Scottish connections and settings contrasted with far-flung counterweights that gave us the balance we desired. True, there were a fair number of pieces that came close to being accepted but after concentrated discussion and deliberation on the part of the editors, the contents of this anthology is the result. The integrity of our honesty in choices is all we can offer.

If you were accepted – congratulations! If you were rejected, we offer you our commiserations. Always remember, though, that our selections are only our perception of what worked for us. No more and no less. If you read this anthology and are moved then that is all we can ask for: the work will have done its job. As fellow writers, we appreciate you sharing your work with us. We do not say this glibly, as we know it's a special engagement to be able to see new work produced and we value the importance of that part of the writing process.

To focus future submissions on quality rather than quantity, the next issue will have a submission criterion of **one story** or **four poems.** We challenge you to send us your best, finely honed and tightly tuned. Words that dance on the page and seek out our soul.

The next issue is number 25, a milestone in any publication's existence. Let's look to the future and make it one to remember and let's savour the present, sit back, relax, and enjoy *Making Soup in a Storm*.

Valerie Thornton
Brian Whittingham

NEW WRITING SCOTLAND 25

The twenty-fifth volume of *New Writing Scotland* will be published in summer 2007. Submissions are invited from writers resident in Scotland or Scots by birth or upbringing. Poetry, drama, short fiction or other creative prose may be submitted but not full-length plays or novels, though self-contained extracts are acceptable. The work must be neither previously published nor accepted for publication and may be in any of the languages of Scotland.

Submissions should be typed, double-spaced, on one side of the paper only and the sheets secured at the top-left corner. Prose pieces should carry an approximate word-count. **You should provide a covering letter, clearly marked with your name and address. Please do <u>not</u> put your name or other details on the individual works.** If you would like to receive an acknowledgement of receipt of your manuscript, please enclose a stamped addressed postcard. If you would like to be informed if your submission is unsuccessful, or if you would like your submissions returned, you should enclose a stamped addressed envelope with sufficient postage. Submissions should be sent by **30 September 2006**, in an A4 envelope, to the address below. We are sorry but we cannot accept submissions by fax or e-mail.

Please be aware that we have limited space in each edition, and therefore shorter pieces are more suitable – although longer items of exceptional quality may still be included. A maximum length of 3,500 words is suggested. Please send no more than a single short story and no more than four poems.

ASLS
c/o Department of Scottish History
9 University Gardens
University of Glasgow
Glasgow G12 8QH, Scotland

Tel +44 (0)141 330 5309
www.asls.org.uk

Gregor Addison

SLIPPING AWAY

On the bus, a woman is throwing up words in the air like a child with armfuls of leaves. The sun flickers between the buildings on Dumbarton Road and the spaces in between come alive with the rhythms of her speech. Ian rests his head against the window and lets the engine shaking the red drum that surrounds him vibrate through his hollow body. In his head her words are rattling around looking for something to connect with and, suddenly, surprisingly, they find a corner of him that is still alive and that recognises what she is saying.

'It's not what he said that I remember, it's how he made me feel. We used to talk all the time. Sometimes he'd tell me to shut up when we were in bed because I talked all the time. And he made me laugh. But it's how he made me feel that I remember the most.'

Her voice thins the more she speaks. It comes apart and the words drift but her voice refuses to break. It maintains instead its pace, keeping on until the end. The other woman nods and, occasionally, looks out of the window at the passing shapes and the blocks of light. The bus judders at a stop and jars his head against the cold glass until he straightens, dazed.

The other day, at the hospital, had been hard. She was propped up in bed with pillows that still could not give her enough support to meet death face on. The eyes were hollowed out, small like hard black beads, darting in the drawn, wan face that looked to him, anxiously. At the bedside his mother sat and held her hand.

'I don't think there's a drop of blood left in me,' she said, speaking softly now.

Ian noticed that his smile was rigid and mirroring the cold grey tube of the bed frame which his hands gripped. Her hands were heavily veined and bruised like a vine, the drip coloured like a rose stem, but her flesh white and pale and giving way to the bluish tinge of death. He was troubled by how small she now looked in that big overwhelming bed with its heavy, napped sheets. There was nothing left of her, after all.

The years had had her away like crows.

Midday, the day after, coming home by train, he couldn't believe it was over for her. His mother had phoned during the night and told his father she had slipped away. 'Slipped away'. It was as though his mother had fallen asleep by her bedside and woken to find the bed empty, the wards quieted, the floors blued and shining in the pale moonlight that got in through an open window. 'Slipped away'. But everyone knew what it meant. The end to the waiting had come at last. He decided to go back home, to be alone again, to have time to think, to slip away and leave the shared silence for others to digest.

And so, there he was, at midday – on a moving train.

The shore in turmoil with small feeding birds, the cockle strand like a scythe in the river's side, the early sun bleeding into the waves; all of it seemed to tick over uninterrupted, incessant as the small red alarm clock by her bedside. A man walked his dog through the thin blue day; and Ian's eyes, red and sore and all too heavy with life, hung on the fat puffy bluffs of his cheeks. As the train passed Cardross, the trees adopted strangely defensive postures. He felt like a stranger, hoping the rain would sweep down off of those far-flung hills and take him with them. The gnarled hedgerows bent over themselves, fearing the worst.

A black plastic bag wrestled with the wind and collapsed in a water-filled ditch and sank almost from sight, but for its soft back clinging to the surface without breaking through. There were syringes on the line. Each time Ian closed his eyes, he felt the vertigo. Submerged shapes in the sand pushed up into the daylight; an oil drum, half a tyre, encrusted concrete blocks armoured with mussels and the occasional stubborn limpet that didn't know when to let go. At Bowling, there were rotten hulks of ships that clung to the memory of a boat, dark and drear, almost swallowed whole by the silted-up basin. The red of the clouds made him want to take a knife and cut the underbelly of the day and deflate it, hauling out the stillborn carcass from within, delivering it dead to some other expectant passenger.

He rested his tired, thought-filled head against the glass and listened to the electric hum in the overhead cables. She was gone. Everything was as it was before, but she was gone.

*

On the bus, Ian listened to the woman's words.

'... it's how he made me feel that I remember the most,' she said. She looked out of the window.

The other woman agreed.

'You never think the moment will come.'

She spoke to comfort herself against her loss, to keep away the hard edges, and kept the constant flurry of words up, filling the air with them so that she didn't have to let the silence in. The words were good, they filled her mouth and stopped it drying up; they let her eyes forget their work and stopped them having to look and decipher and anticipate and predict. Perhaps, if Ian hadn't been alone, he too would have kicked up piles of leaves and scattered fragments of memories across the heads of the other passengers, would have showered them with wonders of motherhood and courage; how she gave instructions even at the end, ordered others to action, told them what they must do; saw it coming and fixed her weakened gaze squarely on death. He couldn't understand why she was not afraid. And now, he thought about how she made him feel, thought of the scones and the soup, the criticism and the advice, and let himself rest in the falling leaves and the autumnal shards of orange, red and yellow light that scattered dizzily, easily, around him.

Colin Begg

THERE IS NO MONEY IN POETRY?

The enterprising bard of Lochranza
ran a poetic extravaganza
folk gathered round
and bought lines for a pound
or a discount of four quid a stanza.

Laura Bissell

AND WHEN I OPENED MY EYES

And when I opened my eyes she was there and she said
hurtful things to me like
'I love you very much and I will never leave you'
And silly things like
'I hope that we will never be apart'

I answered with an angry statement such as
'Thank you for everything you have ever done for me'
And humorous things like
'Please don't ever go away'

She responded with an agitated
'I hope that you are very happy and contented and never
want for anything ever'
I replied despondently
'I will be as still as an icy spot on the road'

She then asked
'I hope that you will remember me as a sunny day or a
rainy one'
I answered in the terms of the weather
'Fridays will be the hardest'

She asked coldly what I thought about things like love and
the weather
And I answered that the weather was cold today and that I
loved her

She looked weathered and lovely and like a cold and
melting snowman in the snow that is turning to slush with
a little bit of sun on it

I asked her venomously what time it was
She answered 'I hope you remember the things I told you
about the dangers of damp and the perils of the ice'

I answered 'I shall never ever take sweets from a snowman,
nor shall I ever leave a pram outside a sweet shop in case
bicycle thieves mistakenly take the baby'

She said, 'I am glad you remember the rules of love that I taught you when we both hit forty'

I laughed and said 'It was a shame we had to climb that hill alone I wanted to toboggan with you to the bottom'

She answered in a stage whisper 'REMEMBER THE TIME WE SKIDDED ON THE ICE ON THE ROAD AND HIT AN ICE CREAM VAN AND THE 99'S AND 100'S WENT ALL OVER THE ROAD AND LEFT A POOL OF BLOOD IN THE SNOW AND IT SEEPED IN AND WAS COVERED IN HUNDREDS AND THOUSANDS AND MILLIONS AND THEN THE VAN MELTED'

I responded in haste with a statement such as
'I hope we don't have to clean up any of the messes we make in this life it would take me a week just to do one for example the milk I spilt in terms of my love life between 1987 and the summer of 1989'

She muttered 'I hope that the rain always washes away my tears'

I answered condescendingly 'I think they have dishwashers and microwaves for those sorts of things now and other things with plugs and wires and things that also need extension leads that I never have and never will buy'

She asked if I could pass her the ice and I lashed out with 'I hope you realise that a storm is coming and that the washing is still on the line'

She responded in scientific terms and told me that worrying has become obsolete and that these things will generally come out in time or with a little soda water

I looked surprise and said 'I never thought the old thing could go so fast'

She asked if she was as old as the earth yet and I said 'You have to become salt first before you can learn to run or walk or drive'

She looked me deep in the eyes and said 'I wish I knew the colour of the next thing'

I said 'I think it is blue like my eyes and the sky when it isn't cloudy'

She said she remembered as a child a long hazy summer of ice cream and swims and sticks poking things that didn't move and I told her not to be silly that she was not alive in the time of those things and that she should forget about it mister

Norman Bissell

A MACKEREL SKY
for Birgit

Back then they too
sat on this beach
and watched the falling sun
they left their dun
high above the bay
and came here
with thin beakers
to sup and to marvel
at the energy of crashing waves
the steady flow of tides
forever turning
and at the sky
a mackerel sky
the fishermen call it
ribbed clouds stretching south
gold fading to bloody red
slowly dimming to grey
and the blueness behind
steadily turning silver,
of course they came here
they had fewer distractions
and were part of
these waves
and this sky
as are we.

LONE SEAL TRAVELLING SOUTH

It was the kind of night when midges flitted
all ways in the windless night air
their wings transparent in golden sunlight
and sparrows whirred softly past
as you sat at your front door,
a lazy quietness taking hold of the place
and the village at peace with itself.
On such a night I took myself off to the shore
to catch another luminous sunset over Mull
and as I sat overlooking the calmest of calm bays
a lone seal came following the coast at dusk
travelling south along the Luing shore
every so often leaping out of the water
ducking down and with a flip disappearing
deep into that liquid world of fish and clams
and all that seals dream of
to emerge further south along the coast
moving ever closer to the Ponds
where the big seals hole up on Glas Eilean,
and it was then I took to thinking
of that playful journey home
that we all make alone in the end
wandering the coast leaving no trace
but the lapping of waves on shore.

Jim Carruth

THE BIG MISTAKE

the shepherd on the train told me

is to clip hill milking ewes too soon.

I put my newspaper down;
he'd got my attention.

Nothing puts the milk off them quicker
than just a day like last Wednesday.
And when it goes off at this time of year,
it never comes back.

His warning continues

They never get so rough in the backend,
and have less protection
against the storms and winter chill.

He glances up,
checks his crook in the luggage rack

And another thing
is that the wool neither weighs so heavy
nor looks so well. It's the new growth
that brings down the scales.

A fleece from a ewe that's near
hasn't the same feel as one from a ewe
that has plenty of rise and a good strong stoan.

In the beginning of July the new wool on a thin ewe
will grow more in one week under the fleece
than it will do in three with the fleece clipped off.

He summarised his argument for me

Experienced flock masters never clip hill stocks
before the second week of July.
In terms of the sheep's sufferings
a strong sun is little less severe than a cold rain.

He stopped there
looked out the window at the passing fields
then fell asleep to Waverley
content that a stranger in a suit
had listened to his wisdom
this wisdom I now share with you.

Ian Crockatt

VIKING SPRING

This: barley green as grass
   swaying in gusty May;
its clouds of brandished blades.
   This: ghost-blurs from the coast,
hoar-brained crows cawing, haar
   fingering the halting
hearts and limbs of lambs
   willed to life on the hill.

And this: wing-whirr of geese,
   wind-arrows in narrow
formation confirming
   sea-currents still foment
their baleful heat, hot blood
   and gold-greed still breed in
the mind; sea-wolves still found
   fine steel in hearts: yours; mine.

Tracey Emerson

APRIL

April is rearranging her knickers. In the queue at the garden centre cafeteria. Her hand is right down the back of her tracksuit bottoms, tweaking and twitching and pulling the gigantic pants up and up and up.

'Leave those for now, sweetheart.'

Around us, it's all understanding smiles and knowing looks but we're holding up the line. Behind us, a garden centre worker in dark green dungarees is itching to get at the bacon rolls.

'What do we fancy today?' April is nearly blind and hasn't spoken a word in her entire life but I ask anyway.

She remains engrossed in her underwear, lifting up her jumper now and pulling at her grey, fraying bra.

I snap. I grab her hands away and pull down the jumper.

'Do you want a cup of tea or do you want to go home?'

There's nothing wrong with her comprehension. We shuffle along the counter, picking up a raspberry slice and a pot of tea for one.

I feel guilty. On a good day, I might see the situation from April's point of view and dredge up some patience. Sometimes, her knicker elastic cuts into her like barbed wire and none of her clothes feel right and all she wants to do is take them off and hit her head with her hand until it all makes sense. But this is not a good day. The sky is all grey probability. Possibility is blue.

April pulls on my arm as we wait to pay. A sign of anxiety. She is desperate to complete her money routine. Routines make her feel safe. Every Tuesday morning it's always the same.

I'll arrive at her house and her hand's in my face until a nurse brings us money.

I give her a pound – the same pound I have to prise out of her hand when we get to the till.

Transaction complete – her hand's out again, smacking against me until I give her the change.

'There we are April, all done,' I say.

God I want to scream. Scream until she takes her dirty, persistent hands off me.

At least we're accepted here. This garden centre welcomes the excluded. Mothers with young children, the disabled, the elderly, all of them have permission to be as noisy and crippled and senile as they like. It can look like the best or the worst of humanity, depending on the mood you're in.

I find a table for two, helping April into the seat with no one behind it. That's important because at the exact moment she swallows her last mouthful of tea and cake, she'll shove her chair back and stagger away from the table, pulling at me to take her home. We had a near miss with a toddler in a pushchair last month.

April's hands stretch out for the tray, which I pull away from her. I cut the cake into quarters – otherwise she'd down it in one – and pour her a milky tea with two sugars.

I push the tea and cake over to April and bring her hands in contact with them. She begins to investigate the raspberry slice. I know she can't see what she's eating but it's disgusting. She's squishing the pink fondue centre between her fingers, nervously dabbing it onto her tongue. Next she'll start on the thick chocolate topping and shortbread base.

An elderly lady waves and smiles at us. A Tuesday morning regular. Every week she brings her dribbling husband in his wheelchair and feeds him tea out of a beaker. So much smiling, so little to smile about.

April is still picking. I can't stand it.

'Just get on with it please, April.'

A guy in baggy jeans and a grey hooded sweatshirt stands opposite us in the Kids' Corner. He's heating a baby bottle in the microwave. He knows I'm looking at him and treats me to a grin. Is he flirting? He knows how desirable he is – young, good looking and most importantly in possession of a child. A baby can make even the dullest man appealing.

He exaggerates the mime of testing the milk temperature, shaking his head and putting the bottle back in the microwave. He looks over again. Perhaps it's not fun but pity his eyes are full of. Does he think he could give me the life I don't have?

April waves her empty teacup in my face. I refill it.

The proud father swaggers away. April's autopsy of the

first piece of cake is complete so she crams the others down her throat as fast as she can, lubricating them with mouthfuls of tea. She coughs with her mouth open. The sight of the tea and crumb sludge makes me feel sick. I want to reach over the table and force her revolting mouth shut.

'Take your time, April, take your time.' I keep my tone kind and patient.

Two middle-aged couples sitting to our left stare approvingly at our odd tableau. I'm used to that. A pretty, compassionate girl helping the 'special' person. It's an enticing illusion.

'How does she do that, bless her?' they might say.

I pretend. Like everybody else. And when a stranger looks at me I remember the role I'm playing and how I'm supposed to be feeling and it helps me carry on. Just like the guy at the microwave, pretending he doesn't lie awake at night, hating his child for the noise coming out of it. Or the old woman, pretending she's never wanted to take her husband and his wheelchair to the top of a hill and simply let go.

Hazel Frew

HUNGRY SWANS

From choppy waters
Come translucent feet
Graceful over pebbles
Membranes flattening
onto sea debris like
Smooth wet netting.

Winding their long necks
toward us
Slowly and surely
approaching
Emerging upright
Pedestrians of the sea
Plump marionettes
held by invisible thread.

We feed bread
to these dappled swans
Throwing crumbs
up into the air
For the acrobatic gulls
who catch effortlessly

Across the bay
a lighthouse blinks
Winking at the cold day
A lifeboat bobs
in the water

All is tranquillity
As the river stretches
her legs out to sea.

William Gilfedder

DIPLOMATIC COUP OVER THE CANAPÉS

After attending a more than usually boring Embassy
cocktail party
And listening to a drunken diplomat
Bragging about how he has fairies at the bottom of his garden
The Egyptian Ambassador was heard to remark
'Well that may be all very fey and other-worldly
But of course back home in Cairo
We have Pharaohs at the bottom of ours'

Touché.

Paul Gorman

BEHIND THE SCENES AT THE PUPPET THEATRE

Alan Day, a plumber of fifteen years, had a finger jammed in an old lady's cold water pipe when he decided to start his own puppet theatre. Fiona, his wife, was concerned. Alan was unwilling, when she pressed him, to examine the reasons for such a tangential change of occupation. With a humility that nagged her like an unreachable itch, he simply shrugged and gave thanks to whatever benevolent force had guided him to his new vocation.

He was soon in the grip of a compulsion. He bought books, tools, materials. He visited libraries and websites. He phoned experts and visited real puppeteers and theatres. He refitted the back of his van, laid strips of carpet in the back and built a portable, collapsible theatre-box. It was large enough for him to crouch in, but small enough to erect in a front room. Burgundy drapes framed a drawstring curtain, behind which was a backdrop he painted himself and which altered depending on the story being played out. He painted the name of his new concern in proud white lettering upon the dark green panels of his van. Adverts were placed in the local newspaper. He spent every day shaping papier mâché glove puppets in the upstairs room that he and Fiona always hoped would someday become a nursery. The All-Day-Long Puppet Theatre was born.

It didn't take long for the phone to ring. Kids have birthdays, and some of the lucky ones have parties. The luckiest of all have magicians perform, or clowns, or puppet-shows.

And what of the puppets themselves?

When Fiona asked to see his secret creations, Alan declared that Punch and Judy belonged to a distant era, one which bore no resemblance to the complex world inhabited by today's children.

Superheroes, he decided, were what children liked. He had seen the cartoons and the toys that they enjoyed. With Fiona as his test audience, he set the theatre up in their living room. The curtain rose in jolts and jerks and from somewhere a tinny amplifier crackled into life. The show began.

Alan massaged his thighs afterwards with the heel of his palm. A tiny superhero, painted bright pink, dangled from the other hand, arms flailing helplessly about a wrinkled head.

–What did you think?

–I liked the one that looked like a bear.

–You mean Supercat?

–But I wasn't so sure about that one. She pointed to the pink figurine in his hand. He held it up and the arms flopped to its sides.

–The Mighty Pig?

–It looks like a penis.

Alan bit his lip. –What about the performance?

–It was fine. They beat the hell out of each other, just like a real Punch and Judy show.

When the day of the first booking arrived, long circled on the kitchen calendar, he drove off full of enthusiasm. The back of the van was stuffed with puppets and the foldaway theatre.

But Alan had misjudged.

Fiona found him at the kitchen table when she came home. He stared at the tabletop, and picked absently at the stitching of Supercat's costume.

–The kids were bored. The parents too. They didn't want superheroes. Someone even put the TV on instead. He brandished the semi-naked puppet. –And they're not really super. How do you give a papier mâché pig X-ray vision?

Weary, Fiona sat down opposite him. He'd clearly been home a while, but hadn't started to prepare dinner.

–What about panto characters? Puss in Boots? Cinderella? Then you have a storyline you can play with.

–At Christmas, maybe. His tone was dismissive. –What I need is to put more detail into them; more life. Flesh them out. Put more of me into them.

His footsteps thumped as he bounded up the stairs. Beside the table lay a scattered pile of primary-coloured rags, their seams all unpicked.

When she called to him that his tea was getting cold, the fevered chipping of wood could be heard from upstairs. She heard it again when she went to bed, putting her head around the door. The anglepoise light illuminated her husband's hands. They moved with a life of their own, pulling shapes from wood. She loved his hands; large but dextrous and expressive. She longed to touch them.

–Goodnight.

Alan didn't look up.

–Will the children understand the French?

When Alan spoke, the puppet on display moved in emphasis.

–He won't really talk in French, just wiz an eavy agzent, like zis. His catchphrase is a sort of 'aw-*haw*'. He'll be funny.

On the stage, Fiona watched Alan's latest, and favourite, creation: Monsieur Amour. He was a dark, seemingly greasy-haired Casanova, with a thick black moustache.

–It's just gloss paint. Touch it!

In the days and nights since the first failed performance, Alan had secreted himself in the upstairs room. Fiona no longer called it the nursery.

He emerged with a second batch of puppets. Some were clearly superheroes with a fresh coat of paint and assumed identities.

–He's got a dark past, you see. He waggled the Gallic lover from side to side. –I've got a whole back story for him. Besides, he has to be French. 'Mister Love' would sound rubbish.

–Right ...

–What I want is eyebrows that'll really move.

–Will children laugh at him?

–He's even got a bunch of flowers I can put in his hand, or a box of chocolates I made out of a matchbox.

–But will children laugh at him?

–Grown-ups will. But there's slapstick too. The flowers conceal a water-pistol!

Fiona rubbed wearily at her eyes. It was after midnight, and she'd been waiting until the paint was dry so Alan could demo his latest routine. She started work at the factory in six hours.

–Show me it, then.

Bookings slowly accumulated; every week Alan arranged the advert in the paper, and he began to talk about taking bookings over the web.

–But the show's the thing. I don't want to keep doing the same stuff. I've got to keep it fresh, he explained. Fiona returned one afternoon to a table covered with designs for new puppets. No pans bubbled on the hob; no smells of cooking warmed the house. She dropped her bag and began noisily slamming cupboard doors. There was no reaction from her husband, who returned to his drawings.

–Don't the kids just want the same old routine? You know how they laugh at the same joke over and over.

–But these are better characters. He shifted in his seat like an excited schoolboy. –More nuance. More personality. More reason to exist. He brandished a sheet of paper covered in sketchings. Fiona took it from him. Ed the Ned, dressed in sportswear and a tiny Burberry baseball cap; a miniature gold chain about his acne-studded throat.

–I don't know about this.

–Trust me!

Fiona tried to imagine his audience, a semicircle of open, expectant faces, and pictured the scared bewilderment creeping across them. Still, she supposed he must be doing enough right, for the bookings continued to grow. Every evening he spent upstairs designing, molding, chiselling, painting, stitching or writing. His troupe had grown to almost twenty. After each performance he raved only about how to improve. Fiona suspected he had fallen prey to that most modern of conditions – the lust for fame. She put it to him one night as he read from his latest script.

–You're really up yourself these days, you know that?

He shifted onto an elbow. –Does it bother you? I know I spend quite a lot of time fiddling with them.

–Just spend some time fiddling with me for a change.

–Okay! He made to leap from the bed. –I've got just the idea!

–No!

Alan froze, pale and exposed.

–No puppets.

He clambered back into bed and snapped off the light.

Fiona came home from work with the warmth of a Chinese takeaway rising from a thin polythene bag. The oven was on, and the kitchen warmed by it. She peered inside. The face of a papier mâché puppet drying on a baking tray gazed back at her with wide, pupil-less eyes. Alan was in the lounge, surrounded by a stack of rented DVDs. *The Godfather*, Parts I and II; *Raging Bull*; *Taxi Driver*. For the impressionable minds of his audience, she hoped that this wasn't research into plot lines. *Apocalypse Now*; *Last Tango in Paris*. She scooped this last title from the pile and the whole edifice clattered to the floor.

–What's this?

–Method. Method acting. It'll get me *closer*.

That night, Fiona took the initiative and they made love for the first time in months. Alan, as usual, was silent until his moment of climax when he uttered, to Fiona's alarm, a soft but unmistakable 'aw-*haw*' in the manner of Monsieur Amour. She climbed off him.

–I'm not fucking a puppet, she spat. But, she thought as he retreated to the little room, maybe I am.

–Is there anybody in there? Fiona called one night, rapping knuckles on his skull. He blinked and ushered her away. She stood on the threshold of the little room and surveyed his factory. After a moment he sensed her continued presence and turned to look at her. The body language was clear. She left the door ajar.

His interest in other things withered. He no longer seemed to possess opinions, but listlessly assented to Fiona's every suggestion. She booked a late holiday to Spain for a week in which there were no theatre bookings. In the shade of the apartment, Alan lounged in the depths of a silence Fiona mistook as relaxation. When they returned – two pale, silent, distant individuals peering out of the same tiny sphere – the allure of the power she held over him evaporated. She, too, slumped into a torpor. She began to dread coming home from work, but couldn't muster the energy to either escape with her colleagues on a Friday night, or to walk out.

She didn't leave. But they no longer argued: Alan gave in to every one of her demands, pleas, ideas or criticisms if it allowed him to continue undisturbed. And the less they argued, the less they indulged in energetic sex to make up afterwards. Fiona knew that somewhere there must still reside a sexual drive that wasn't being diverted into puppet-making, if she could only tease it to the surface.

One evening, eager to pump vigour into their deflating relationship, she smuggled a pricing gun home from work, as used in shops to affix price-stickers to tins of food. It seemed to work. Tentative at first, they covered each other with tiny price tags and peeled them off one by one. The adhesive clung painfully, deliciously, to the body's fine hairs. When the gun had served its purpose and they wrestled on the bed, she had a momentary vision that Alan's face was only a mask, a papier mâché facade moving above her, with nothing of substance beneath. She clawed at his throat, plunged her nails into the skin and to her satisfaction he yelped, in pain or delight. He was real; he did exist; he had substance, still. She slept afterwards, exhausted but reassured.

One evening, they lay beside each other on the sofa, watching a film. Alan had, in his cryptic words, been

–experimenting with motors

for reasons he didn't divulge. He stomped downstairs, muttering without coherence about the failure to get them to conform to his plan. Fiona suggested he take his mind off puppets. Wearily, he assented.

The lights were turned off and the room was lit sporadically with the ghostly glow of the TV. Fiona sensed him studying her profile.

–What are you doing?

–Looking at you. I've not looked at you properly for ages.

She giggled, and burrowed into him like sand.

–You're making me nervous.

He toured a finger down the length of her nose. She opened her lips in expectation but the fingers moved across the arc of her nostrils instead.

–And now what are you doing?

–Just looking at your face, he said.

She purred. –That's nice.

Even badly fitting clothes will, in time, hug the skin in a familiar way. So Fiona was used to the nightly retreat of her husband. His obsession still burned. Still he drafted ideas, and now he spoke in different voices as he fleshed out new characters.

It was weeks since he had shown her any new routines.

She realised now, stirring a lonely cup of tea before she left for work, that she missed what interaction his trial runs had brought. Despite everything, she enjoyed seeing the new puppets. Some were based on characters from film or fairy-tale but others were clearly the offspring of a hitherto suppressed imagination. Whether the shows he produced for his paying audiences resembled the screen tests in the front room she had no idea. The bookings still came in; never quite enough, but they came. And still he worked, driven to endlessly create new puppets, new characters, new stories.

At the weekend they had gone to a DIY superstore. Fiona dreamed of new bathrooms, a new kitchen. Alan bought a drill.

–For my new project, he said.

She didn't ask, and now wished she had. Their relationship had not deteriorated to such a point that he wouldn't show off his work like an eager schoolchild, so it had to be something big taking all his time. Something ambitious. She gulped her tea and crept upstairs. Slowly, she turned the handle and pushed. The door didn't budge. Then she noticed the keyhole. Since yesterday morning he'd put a lock on the door. With, she supposed, the new drill. She slipped back down the stairs and out of the house. The cool morning mist sizzled against the raging heat of her face.

She walked home that evening with a man from work. She wasn't even sure of his name. Jim, was it, or John? They walked the streetlit roads to her house. He lived nearby. As they approached, he told a joke and her laughter collapsed into sobs. She wiped at her eyes.

–What's the matter?

–Nothing.

She couldn't remember the last time she'd laughed. Not the polite or expedient chuckles people made at work, but a real, heartfelt, natural laugh.

–This is me. She searched in her bag for housekeys.

–I'll see you tomorrow, then? he asked.

–Yes. She raised a hand as if to wave, but instead hurried into the house. She blew her nose and blinked her eyes clear before calling out.

–I'm home!

–I know.

She jumped. He was standing in the open doorway of the front room.

–Who was that?

–Just one of the guys from work.

–What's his name?

–I don't know.

–You don't know? Alan's tone was flat, but she was alert to the emotion it suppressed.

–I was only walking with him, having a laugh. You know, a laugh?

–I know I've maybe been a bit distant but—

–But what? You think I'm having an affair? Don't you think I'd have done that by now, for all I get out of you? I'd be as well sleeping with one of your puppets.

–After everything I've tried to do.

–What? What have you done except shut yourself up in that room?

Alan lunged towards her and grabbed her by the wrist.

–Come with me.

–Let go!

To her surprise, he released his grip. He glared at her and she followed him up the stairs.

–Weeks I've spent on this. He dug in his pockets for the key. –Wait there, I'll bring it out. It's almost finished.

–I'm your wife, not a kid! Fiona shouted at the slowly closing door.

–Just wait a second, his voice came muffled from inside.

The door was hauled open. A tiny puppet, shrouded in a blanket, nestled in his arms. He cradled it as if fragile, lowered his voice when he hissed at her.

–See! This is what I've been making. For us. For you. He thrust the bundle at her. She held it away from her breast like a mangy cat. –A baby, for us; a real baby. The anger, the jealousy, was passing. The breathlessness in his voice was eagerness now, spilling over. Fiona felt like she'd been punched in the gut.

The puppet's eyes opened. Eyes the colour and shape of Fiona's own looked up at her. The tiny peach-coloured jaw moved with the awkwardness of a key turning a rusted lock.

–Mama, it said.

Rody Gorman

OISEAN

Nuair a thill Oisean
An dèidh trì cheud bliadhna
Na bhothan a-staigh sna h-Eileanan Seunta,
Cha b' e ruith ach leum leis
Bonn a leagail air fonn a dhùthchais
Far an robh Pàdraig
Agus a chuideachd a' feitheamh.

Cho luath 's a leag,
Nach ann a chrom e sìos an aois.
Thuit na faclan far a chraois
Is na sùilean far a chinn.
B' ann air èiginn a rinn e 'n gnothach
Air èigheachd a-mach ri clàr an eich:
Teich, an ainm an àigh! An ainm Nì Math, teich!

TUATH

Ciaradh an fheasgair a chaidh
An tuath a reic,
Shuidh sinn a-staigh ri lic an teinntein.

Dh'fhàg e fhèin a churrac
Air a' bhòrd chruinn, làmhan còmhla,
Sùilean a' sgeannadh air an dealbh gun fhaicinn.

Thug i fhèin crùbadh don fhear mhòr mu dheireadh
Thall is a-bhos, na deòir
A' tuiteam don làr shalach.

Dh'èirich e air
A chasan mu dheireadh, chuir air a *mhac* aosta
'S dhruid an doras-beòil na dhèidh.

Charlie Gracie

STORM

martins
soar
blackly swoop
in the gathering grey
the chirp chirp of them
stings the air
the frip of their wings
as they steal bugs from the evening sky

tomorrow
it will thunder

then
the air will be clear

ON CARN DEARG

The green weed waves
like a dead girl's hair.
A green-haired girl
lost in the clear mountain burn.

She flows down around my feet
as I drink her in.
My hands stroke her hair
as she quenches me.

And on we walk
through the rough heather
and over the quiet red rock
and onto the wind-flattened top.

Lis Lee

PEBBLE

The pebble had a hole,
a white quill stuck there
like a finger in an ear,
silencing wind.

A gull can't fly if stones
deafen its feathers,
pin them down,
caulk them with tar.

Oil tankers ease over,
punctured in storms
that drove flight
through a stone's eye.

Joanna Lilley

INUKSHUK

The Inuit
mimic
human
forms with chunks of permafrosted granite.
Stand them on tundra outcrops,
as morbid   signposts
to trap   the caribou
so they   can capture,
eat and   wear them.

Andrew McCallum

THE BALLAD O PAW BROON

Paw Broon's traikin alang a street,
whaes waas are blin, save
fur the twa-three bricks that let us
 see it's a waa;
a shelpit wee skelf o a man gaun
 hame frae e's wark,
jaiket dreipt owre dungarees,
bunnet stapt ticht an drookit doon
 owre e's croon,
the maakins o a Friedrich Nietzsche tash
 curt'nin e's mou.

E birls intae a close
an sterts the lang sclimb o the stairs,
God's last lauch at the end o a lang sair day.
E swithers oan the stairheid an
 swallaes a sigh,
afore pittin e's haun tae the haun'le
an pushin open the door.

They're aa therr,
Joe, Hen, Daphne an Maggie,
Horace, the twins, an the nameless bairn,
an Maw, tae the bield o whaes muckle breists
the hale faim'ly's ingethert,
an Grandpaw reekin in the coarner
 ahint e's pipe.

An they're aa fechtin.
Daphne an Maggie hae a grup o
 ane anither's hair;
Joe haes Hen in a heidlock;
Horace's specs are hingin frae ane lug,
 e's neb bluidin;
an the twins are paddlin at ane anither lik
 twa bantamwaichts;
Maw's skelpin the bairn,
an Grandpaw's roarin thaim oan.

An sumpin snaps.
Paw caa's the table owre an stauns
pechin in the middle o the flair.
'A'm lookin fur some peace an quait,'
        e beals.
'Is it owre much fur a man tae ask,
that's bin knockin e's pan oot
        aa day?'

Jaws drap.
Maw's haun freezes in mid-skelp.
Then aa thir faces thaw tae a sleekit grin.
'Yer lookin fur some peace an quait,' says ane.
'Huv ye loast it, like?' speirs anither.
'Whaur did ye see it last?'
'Huv ye looked in the press?'
'Or mebbe ablow yer kip?'
'Are ye shair it's no unner yer bunnet,
or in yer pipe, ye bletherin auld skyte?'
An the fechtin faas tae lauchter.

'Hae ye's no heared?' Paw gaffs thaim
wi a glance. 'Waatkin's deid,
an we hae kilt 'im, ya bampots!'
An e whauks e's bunnet tae the flair
        in disgust.

Silence faas lik a stane. Then,

'Michty me!' Maw gasps,
wi a haun tae er hert. 'Help,
murder, polis! Daes that mean ... ?'

'Aye,' says Paw, soopin the room wi e's airm.
'Ye're aa waashed up, din,
        "under erasure".'

An birlin roon, Maw sees
er bairnies fade tae scribblins,
        ane bae ane,
an then thir ootlines melt tae naethin,
leavin nocht but speech-bubbles in the air,
cryin 'Jings!' 'Crivvens!' 'Help ma boab!'
        til they pop tae.
An Maw's peenie faas emp'y tae the flair.
An Grandpaw spontaneously combusts.
An Paw haes peace an quiet at last.

Later oan, doon the pub,
Paw breenges in, the warse o drink,
an tells aa-buddy wha'll listen tae'm
        hoo e settilt thir hash.
'An whit's Auld Scotia noo,' e slavers,
'if no the tomb an sepulchre o
        the couthy.'

('Ach, awaa an shite!' growls wee Shug,
        sittin in the coarner,
                nursin a drink, an
                        contemplatin a thistle.)

Stuart Robert Macdonald

ECLIPSE

Wind patterns woven
through green grass

you and I
shared the common
enemy called aggrievement
the time an
old blue train
got stuck on
the east coast
line heading home

dead bracken like
caramel frost crystals

and then when
the train nudged
into Prestonpans the
conductor told us
to get off
as it started
to sleet and
there was nowhere
near to shelter

slender bare saplings
straight as spears

it is way
past modesty now
but when the
sun came out
the cold garment
of our shadows
fell from us
landing together in
a pile creating
a small night
for our feet

and the gibbous
moon waxing alone

we waited for
the connecting bus
clouds passed overhead
and in the
time it took
the sun to
blink we were
stranded in twilight

hanging by a
thread of shivers

WHILST I WAS AWAY ACROSS THE BRINY

(I)

A kind letter
sits mat happy
ocean flat

caught like a falling sea star
miles from dry eyes

(II)

three love letters
shoal along
the sea-bedded hall

praying like lonely hunters
miles from star light

(III)

a note of bleeding hearts
flutters from
hands across shining seas

drifting starward
miles from daylight's anchor

(IV)

One tender lyric
rests upon
salt sea piles

glowing brighter
miles from time and tide.

Frank McHugh

HOME COMFORTS
Tsunami – Boxing Day '04

White plastic chairs and concrete blocks
Flood through the screen and onto
My living-room carpet.
A woman, washed under my Christmas tree,
Lies bruised and calling, I think,
For her children –
Two of whom lie lifeless behind the couch.

My wife sobs, my children haven't noticed
As the sea water, greyed and woody,
Reaches the stairs,
And the damp stench of nature
Creeps, unsmiling, around my house.

The next wave flings through a man
Who hangs on to the leg of my kitchen table
But loses his grip and flies, screaming,
Through the back door.

Then, exotic quiet and warm breeze stillness.
The woman bobs against the skirting,
Her brightly coloured skirt sodden,
Clinging to her legs.
Among the detritus,
A photo album and a puffer fish.

WINDOW PAIN

On wet and windy November nights
When the earth is hung with purple drapes
A leaf-strewn Good Friday altar,
I feel the pang of the motherless.
Like a bruise on my heart,
I picture some tramp under a well-kept hedge
And, slipping into his skin,
Feel his thin, wet cover and
It feels like a family death in my childhood –
A cold vinyl seat reflecting
The fear of forever with neither father nor mother.

Màrtainn Mac an t-Saoir

SAMHAIN AIG BBC BREAKFAST

Nuair nach tàinig
aon chaileag bheag bhrèagha
no bòcan de ghille borb
air chèilidh
air Oidhche Shamhna,
an dèis dhi
am poca mòr shuiteas
aig Sainsbury's
a chàradh air a maide-buinn,
mar bhalla-dìon làn ùbhlan
dha a cogais choimhearsnachd,
chuir reul na moch-mhaidne
dhith a h-aghaidh choimheach,
thug i na tuirneapan beaga
às a cluasan
is le osna
anns an robh guth a màthar
stob i dà mhini-Mars bar
na bus.

Gun dad dhem mìlsead
a sgrìobadh far fiaclan foirfe
mhùch i solas nan naoi uairean
is ghuidh i air na mairbh
dhol nan naoimh bheusach.

SAMHAIN FOR BBC BREAKFAST

When not a single
pretty little girl
or an unruly spectre of a boy
came guising
on Halloween night,
after she had placed
the large packet of sweets
from Sainsbury's
on the threshold,
like a protective wall of apples
for her community conscience,
the early morning star
took off her false face,
removed the little turnips
from her ears,
and with a sigh
which contained her mother's voice
stuffed two mini-Mars bars
into her cheeks.

Without scraping
any of their sweetness
from perfect teeth
she quashed the nine o'clock light
and beseeched the dead
to become modest saints.

BRISTE NO A' CHISTE?

'S e am foghar-faothachaidh an Dùn Èideann
a ghabh rim thàrrsainn
às òraid an sgoileir ainmeil

eudailean àraid air
bhidio, beul is gnùis
on chladh Ghàidhlig.

Tè a bha am Boston
fad leth-cheud bliadhna is
an 'l' leathann aice cho làidir
's a bha e a' chiad latha a bhlais i
air brochan lom 'Lurain Luathchasaich' air glùin a seanar.

Bodach a bhiodh a' dannsa,
o chionn dìreach bliadhna no dhà,
is e ag aithris 'Diluain, Dimairt',
fhathast air chomas uilinn a ghluasad – le taic nan
 sìdhichean.

Agus a' cheist: an can iad 'bòdhach' am Barraigh?
Oir sin a bh' aig Flòraidh seach 'bòidheach',
na h-isean aig 79 is a thogadh an àite cho fìor iomallach
ann an Ceap Breatann,
nach robh aice ach an tuiseal tabhartach a' startadh na sgoile
 aig seachd.

Seadh, bha faothachdh san fhoghar dhomh
ged a bha na duilleagan àlainn dathte
a' torradh gu trom mum adhbrannan.

Dh'fhòn mi dhachaigh.
Bha Canada air mo chumail na b' fhaide na bha còir.

Guth beag beò a bhruidhinn rim mhobile.
'Fhios agad dè a th' ann airson dìnneir?
Banana air a phasgadh ann am bacon!'

Ach nuair a ràinig mi an taigh – car fadalach –
chan fhaicinn ach measan dubha is
geir gheal a' cruadhachadh fodhpa.

'Carson nach do dh'ith thu am biadh annasach?'
dh'fhaighneachd mi dhen tè bhig.

'Sàillibh,' orsa ise gun chùram,
'Cha bu thoigh l' mi e.'

BROKEN OR THE COFFIN?

Edinburgh's autumnal respite
welcomed my fleeing
from the famous scholar's lecture

surprising treasures on
video, mouth and facial expression
from the Gaelic graveyard.

A woman who'd been in Boston
for fifty years
and her broad 'l' as thick
as it was the first day she tasted
Luran Luathchasach's thin porridge on her grandfather's
knee.

An old boy who would dance,
just a few years back,
when reciting 'Monday Tuesday',
still able to move his elbow – with the help of the fairies.

And the question: do they say 'bòdhach' in Barra?
Because that is what Flora used rather than 'bòidheach',
a spring chicken at 79, and raised in such a remote part of
Cape Breton that all she
had was the dative case when starting the school at seven.

Yes, the autumn offered some respite
Although the beautifully coloured leaves
Piled heavily around my ankles.

I called home.
Canada had kept me longer than was appropriate.

A live little voice greeted my mobile.
'Do you know what we're getting for dinner?
Banana wrapped in bacon!'

But when I reached the house – a little late –
I could see only black fruit with
white fat solidifying underneath.

'Why didn't you eat the exotic food?'
I asked my young daughter.

'Because,' she said, unperturbed,
'I not liked it.'

David S. Mackenzie

TÍO

29th September

As Tío becomes more human I'm beginning to detect the fading of my own humanity. Physically, of course, nothing is happening to me; it's Tío who's changing. The gap between us is narrowing and perhaps this is adding to my unease. But the disquiet has been with me from the beginning, from before the beginning. It started the day I conceived the idea of this huge experiment, this grand adventure. Even then, when I was full of joy in the knowledge that I could actually do it, there appeared this inkling of doubt, the feeling that maybe what I was planning to do was morally wrong. Perhaps it was inhuman.

I began the injections four days ago. At first Tío screamed when he saw the needle. He bounced about his cage, swinging across from side to side and chattering away as all chimps do when alarmed. I had to fire a tranquilliser dart into him to slow him down. I didn't give him enough to knock him out cold because I wasn't too sure how the tranquilliser would react with the Promix47. So, just enough to make him sluggish, to lower his resistance. While he was still groggy I gave him the first injection.

There was the chance it would all go wrong, of course. For the next few hours I just sat there by the cage and watched him. After all, he might have had an adverse reaction and perhaps even died. Earlier experiments had resulted in a few casualties. But Tío was OK. When he came round from the tranquilliser he was alert again but subdued. He remained curious – all chimps are curious – but now he seemed more methodical in his curiosity, moving without hurry round his cage, exploring every part of it carefully and systematically as if seeing it for the first time. But then I could be imagining this. I was hoping he would change; that was the whole point. Maybe I saw what I wanted to see. But I don't think so.

For the next three days I followed the same procedure: tranquilliser dart followed by injection. These were quite dull days really. Tío seemed to react in much the same way: the same shuffling around in his cage, examining every last bit of it while I sat outside observing. At quiet times, and they were mostly quiet times, I caught up with my reading. Tío's cage, which is quite big – fifteen feet by ten feet – is set up in my study and pretty much fills it. Next door is the bedroom which, many years ago, I converted into my laboratory. The study's walls are lined with books, many of which I haven't read. Darwin, for example. I'd never quite got round to reading *The Origin of Species*. I did so now.

And it was this afternoon, on the fourth day of the experiment, when I was about halfway through Darwin's great book that I looked up and realised, with something of a shock, that Tío really has changed. A lot.

It's difficult to know how I missed this. Maybe the change actually was gradual, not sudden, but I didn't become aware of it until some kind of threshold had been reached. Anyway, there he was, hanging by his arms halfway up the bars of his cage. He was looking at me, investigating me. He was quiet and seemed very confident, self-assured. I wondered why he preferred this pose, suspended from the bars. Then I looked down and really did get a shock. He wasn't hanging on to the bars at all; he was standing on the floor.

I stood up abruptly and Darwin dropped from my hands. *The Origin of Species* hit the floor in a splash of yellowed pages.

Tío was much taller than before. How could I have missed this? I stepped back. Was he really taller? Yes, of course he was. He was taller because his legs were longer. But this didn't account for all of the change that had occurred and was still occurring. Tío was much straighter, more upright. He no longer had the crouched posture of a chimpanzee; his back was straighter; he was beginning to develop a discernible neck. He was standing tall and erect and I knew that he would never bound around his cage on all fours again; he would walk.

It was time for his injection and he knew this. But, instead of cowering in a corner as he had done before, he pushed his arm through the bars towards me, inviting me, not with resignation, I'm sure, but with something close to desire, to put the needle in his arm.

13th October

That was two weeks ago. Things have moved on since then,

very rapidly, and it's only now that I've had time to write all this down.

On the sixth morning after the start of the injections, it seemed as if Tío was trying to speak. He was producing unusual, non-chimp sounds. I could see that his face had already begun to change, the mouth less prominent, the nose less flat, but I knew that speech would be beyond him, purely on physiological grounds, for some time. He was losing hair, too, I noticed. The floor of his cage had tufts of hair lying about, thick dark hair like short snippets of brown cord, that looked quite alien to the being that was shedding them. His hands were much more human and the strengthening and straightening of his legs meant that he no longer walked on the sides of his feet; his feet were flat on the ground.

Well, Tío, I said, *you're becoming a man.*

Then he said something to me. I couldn't make out what it was but I was sure this was something made up of words, not arbitrary sounds. He was definitely trying to speak. *Tío*, I said to him, *Tío, what are you trying to say?* I repeated: *What are you trying to say?*

Then he said it back to me: *What are you trying to say?* There were some rough edges to the sounds but there was no doubting the words.

I approached the cage and looked directly at him, at his three-quarters-chimp, one-quarter-human face. *Well, well, well*, I said, *I'm absolutely amazed.* His face was sullen, in the way chimps' faces often are, betraying no emotion whatever. *Well, well, well*, he repeated, *I'm absolutely amazed.* And he pushed his arm through the bars ready for the next injection.

I spoke to him for most of the rest of the day. Dutifully he repeated my words. And I have to confess that after a while my wonder at his ability to talk ebbed slightly. Mimicry. That's all it was, really. All chimps are good at this, in gesture and movement, though not, of course, in speech. By the end of that day I was even beginning to weary of Tío's endless repetitions. I wasn't prepared for what happened the next morning.

It was the seventh day. I approached the cage and said, as I had on most mornings: *Good morning, Tío. Are you ready for your injection?* And he replied: *Good morning.* Then he paused. I looked at him and smiled. *Good morning*, I repeated. *Are you ready for your injection?* Any confusion I may have detected in his expression disappeared and, looking directly at me, he said with confidence: *Yes, I am. I'm ready for my injection.*

At that moment it seemed to me there was nothing Tío could do that would astonish me more. But on every day since that morning there have been greater astonishments and further revelations. It's been difficult for me to keep pace with Tío's development, to the extent that I considered discontinuing the injections for a while or at least reducing their frequency. But Tío did not agree to this.

By this time we were talking together quite a lot. And these conversations, though slow at first, were not between master and pupil, they weren't between parent and child; they were between equals. I realise now that after he began talking, I was no longer superior to Tío in any way, if I ever had been.

On the morning after his first unbidden speech he held his arm out for his injection but I said: *No, Tío, not this morning.* When he looked at me then, I could detect an expression in his face for perhaps the first time. It lay somewhere between perplexity and disappointment. *Not this morning, Tío*, I repeated, but he continued to hold his arm out towards me. I could see that nearly all his body hair had disappeared. After a few moments he asked: *Why?*

Because it's not good for you right now, Tío, that's why. Of course I regretted this statement immediately. After all, what I was trying to do was produce an intelligent, thoughtful being, one with a high capacity for enquiry. What I'd said satisfied no one, not even me. And Tío knew it.

Explain, he said, drawing his arm back inside the cage.

Well, you're developing very quickly, I offered, realising as I said this how feeble it sounded. *I mean, you ... I don't want to overstretch things. We need to consolidate*, I said.

Consolidate, he said slowly.

Yes, I said, *it means to pause, to—*

I know what it means, he interrupted.

You do?

Yes.

It was my turn to ask questions. *But how could you*

know? I said. *I haven't used the word. I mean, I haven't said it to you.*

Words are easy, Tío said.

You think so?

Yes. He pushed his arm through the bars again. *They come in through the injections.*

Do they?

Yes. That's why I need them.

Well, I'm sorry, Tío, but not today, I said firmly. And, before he could respond, I turned away and left the room.

I went out for a couple of hours. I thought that wandering round the city might help me to understand what I'd got myself into and what to do next. To my shame, I admit that on that morning, walking the streets of a bright and buoyant city that normally made me feel good to be alive, I thought of destroying Tío. But even as I contemplated this I realised I was using the wrong word. You destroy an animal. Tío wasn't an animal any more. Technically he wasn't human but he was certainly more human than chimpanzee. No, if I wanted to get rid of Tío I couldn't destroy him; I'd have to murder him. And I knew I couldn't do that.

Anyway, when I got home, he was gone.

It shouldn't have surprised me too much, I suppose. His cage was in the centre of a room that wasn't very big. There were objects within reach. No keys, of course, but items that an intelligent being might use to pick a lock. (He told me later he'd used a pair of scissors and some paperclips.)

At first, standing in front of the open cage door, I laughed. I laughed at my own arrogance, the pretension that I could remain in control of this creature of mine. Then, of course, I began to worry. What the hell could I do now? If I called the police, what would I say to them? How could I possibly explain what had happened? No, it was essential to leave the police out of it. The only thing I could do was find Tío myself. As soon as possible.

I was just about to leave the house when Tío returned. There was a uniformed policeman with him.

This gentleman a friend of yours, is he? the policeman asked. He was a tall man but quite portly. I guessed he would be about fifty. He displayed that type of politeness which policemen often have, the sort that's worrying because you suspect it might just be a veneer and it's difficult to decide how thin the veneer might be.

Tío looked at me forlornly. He was wearing a dark blue raincoat which, I assumed, belonged to the policeman. It was a couple of sizes too big for Tío. Not only did he look forlorn, he looked faintly ridiculous.

He's my nephew, I said to the policeman.

Does he often go out stark naked?

When I looked at Tío then, I could see that his facial features were still quite heavy, his brow still a bit craggy, but his nose was slim now, and pointed. He had the lips of a man. He had lost nearly all of his body hair, too. The pale legs that stuck out below the hem of the blue raincoat were hairless. So what was standing before me was a human being.

I realised, Tío said.

What? I asked.

I was on my way home. I realised I was naked.

A bit too late, if you ask me, the policeman said.

My nephew's been under strain, I explained. *He's receiving medical help.*

That doesn't surprise me, the policeman said and he drew a notebook from his top pocket. *I'll need to check*, he added as he searched for a fresh page. *So what's the name of his doctor?*

I hadn't expected this question.

But Tío had. *Dr Prendergast*, he said. *At the Brownlow Practice.*

Is that right? The policeman looked at me. I nodded. Oliver Prendergast was my doctor.

And what's your name? the policeman asked Tío.

Mitchell, he replied. *Alexander Mitchell.*

My name. I nodded again.

Well, Mr Mitchell, I advise you to keep your clothes on in future. And pay attention to your uncle here. He looked at me.

It won't happen again, I said. *I can assure you of that.*

Good. Good. He put his notebook away and accepted his raincoat back from Tío who, naked once more, seemed a little embarrassed.

I'll let it go this time, the policeman said. *But if it happens again ...*

It won't, it won't, I assured him.

OK. He slung his coat over his arm. He looked at Tío. *OK*, he said again. *I'll be off.*

When he'd gone I said: *Well, Tío, things have changed.*

Yes, Tío agreed. *I need some clothes.*

That's not a problem, I said. *I'll get you some.*

He stepped over to the door of the cage and looked inside. *I can't sleep in there any more*, he said. *I'm not a monkey.*

I know, I replied. *You certainly aren't.*

He turned to face me. His voice was confident but his expression made his concern clear. *I need the injections*, he said. *You know that, don't you? You can't stop now.*

I shrugged. *You're right, I suppose.* Then I added: *Yes, of course you're right.*

The project's got to be seen through to its conclusion, he said, *whatever that conclusion might be.*

He was repeating words I had often used. He'd probably heard me saying them. But maybe not. Maybe he'd come up with them all by himself. Or maybe it was just as Tío said: the words came in through the injections. I had no idea how he was learning so quickly but there was no doubt that he was learning. And he was learning everything, not just words. I knew I'd created Tío but my own knowledge of him was diminishing and would obviously decrease further as time went on. Tío's learning would exceed my capacity to keep up with it. But despite this, he was right. We had to go on. *Yes*, I said. *You've convinced me.* And he held his arm out for the next injection.

Over the next week or so we were both very busy. We dismantled the cage in the study and installed a single bed. I went out and bought some clothes for Tío and, in these, he went out and bought some more. His features softened further, became indisputably human. The hair on his head grew and needed to be cut. He disliked the idea of facial hair and began to shave.

And all this time he was learning, learning, absorbing knowledge at an amazing rate. And not just facts, information; he was learning how to express himself, how to interact with other people. It was as if his memory was infinite; he filled it and filled it and still it wasn't satisfied.

He said to me: *Why Tío?* And I told him it meant nephew in Spanish. He corrected me. *It means uncle*, he said. And, of course, he was right. I asked him how he knew. He pointed to one of the bookshelves in the study, the room that was now his bedroom. *I don't sleep much*, he said. *I read.*

I could see a small collection of language primers. I always try to learn a few words of the languages of those countries I visit. *So you speak Spanish, do you?* I asked and, without a trace of irony, he said: *Fluently.*

Of course, what I didn't tell him, but he almost certainly knew, was that I'd been increasing his dosage. All I can say is that I wanted to move on swiftly to a conclusion. I was getting desperate. I didn't know what this conclusion might be but I feared it so I tried to bring it forward and get it over with. I'd made this man who now surpassed his creator in almost every aspect you could name. He was more intelligent than me, more knowledgeable. He held in his head hundreds of times more information than I could ever hope to learn. I suspected that he was wiser than me, too. But then this wasn't difficult. Was I wise who had embarked on this experiment knowing that I might lose control of it? No, I was a bright scientist, keen, single-minded and imaginative. But wise? I don't think so.

And last night the folly of it all was made plain to me. We were talking about the experiment. It was inevitable that Tío would ask me about it. He was sure to examine his genesis one day. And it happened last night, only a few hours ago.

I told him how I'd arrived at the formula for Promix47. It had taken me years, I said, which was true. Eleven years, to be precise. And there had been a few wrong turns along the way, a few mistakes.

Any deaths? Tío asked.

Yes, I'm afraid so, I admitted.

Chimpanzee or human?

I paused. *Two*, I said, *hardly passed the chimp stage but one of them was ... well ... pretty much halfway there, I'd say.*

But you carried on?

Oh yes, I said.

Why?

What could I do but shrug? I said: *Who stops to examine the reasons for doing something when it becomes clear you can actually do it? Any moral questions you might have are swamped by the need to exercise power. The urge to get on with it is just too strong.*

Ambition, he said quietly.

Exactly, exactly, I replied. *All other considerations are overwhelmed by ambition.*

Do you regret it? he asked.

I looked at him then. Tío was a good-looking young man, about twenty-five, and was casually dressed in dark blue jeans and a T-shirt. He was sitting in an armchair adjacent to mine, his elbows resting lightly on the arms. We might have been a couple of friends having a quiet chat.

When I look at you, I said, *then of course not. How could I regret it? You're intelligent – extremely intelligent, in fact – and bright and interested ...*

And human? he asked.

Yes, I said, perhaps too quickly.

Are you sure?

I hesitated. *Well, considering what you were only two or three weeks ago, no, I'm not sure. But then look at you now. How could anyone be in any doubt?*

Anyone but you.

Anyone but me, I agreed reluctantly.

So you still think that I might just be ... what can I say ... a monster? He smiled at me.

There was no use lying. *It's crossed my mind a few times, yes*, I admitted. *How could it not?*

Tío shrugged. *You know what the next experiment is, don't you?* he said.

No, I said. *Tell me.*

Reversal.

From human back to chimp?

Yes.

I shook my head. *It took me eleven years to develop Promix47. It would probably take as long again to come up with the reverse drug.*

I've already done it, Tío said.

I admit, I felt a little afraid just then.

He went on: *It wasn't that difficult. I looked through your lab notes, checked a few things ...*

So you haven't just been reading during the night?

No.

And you mean you've actually done it? You've actually produced the drug?

Oh yes. As I say, it wasn't that difficult. It's through there now. He nodded in the direction of the lab door.

But why on earth would you want to go back? I asked him. *I mean, look at you, look at what you've become. Surely you don't want to go back to being a chimp, do you?*

He looked at the floor. Then he looked up at me and smiled. Faintly. Just the palest imitation of a smile. He was indulging me, I knew. He was pitying a poor, less intelligent being.

That's not quite what I had in mind, he said.

14th October

That was yesterday. I spent today walking round the city, trying to think clearly. But my head was in a daze most of the time. However, when I got home, half an hour ago, exhausted, I had come to a decision. I reached the conclusion I knew I would reach all along.

In a way, it's the perfect solution. Who better to continue my work? Who would I hand everything on to, if not to Tío? The only potential obstacle to his progress is me. There is, in fact, only one small way in which I can help him.

15th October

I had the first injection this morning. I let Tío administer it. He told me that he's not only reversed the formula but streamlined it as well so he expects the changes to be more rapid in my case than in his. Certainly, within an hour I began to feel different. The changes to my body are only just perceptible but they're quite definitely there. My gait is different. My arms and legs feel heavier, more awkward. I'm not sure how but I can feel something moving inside me, something gathering and drawing me in.

On the backs of my hands, more hair. The hands themselves flatter.

Afternoon. The second injection. My knees, my feet.

Tío is rebuilding the cage and I'm unable to help him.

Jane Irina McKie

MEDICINE

I am a hag who drinks with avidity
from rain-filled hoof-tracks.

I haunt bridleways
waiting for wet weather.

I have always done this
since I was an unattractive maid

who found that iron in her diet
assuaged the pain of being shunned.

I suppose in these modern days
I could take Prozac.

I suppose you could say
that I manage my seratonin

with measured sips, or
that lapping from hoof-prints

slakes my appetite for pathos.
Either way, it seems to do the trick.

SPITE-STAKE

If you think your neighbour might
cast the Evil Eye upon your hives,
enervating your bees
or spoiling the taste of your honey,
you must act quickly to construct
a Heath Robinson trap.

It should be a frame or cage
from which to hang
an assortment of bones:
radius and ulna,
hammer and anvil,
the dented skull of a horse.

It should be a spite-stake –
a makeshift nithing-post
like the ones Vikings built
before their battles,
horse-jaws wide agape
to chatter curses at advancing foes.

Iain S. MacPherson

RATHAD NA BEINNE

eadar baile beag sa Bheinn
is Baile Searlot thall,
bhon t-sneachd os cionn fhàsach
is sneachd air bhàrr chuan,
thig fuachd na chnàmhan
is teas na h-aodann

's an dithis aca sin –
Ottomanach air imrich
is tè òg à bail'-iasgaich –
sùilean
a' laighe air a chèile

stadaidh iad
's nochdaidh rathad an teaghlaich
agam fhìn,
air a ghearradh tro chraobhan
is ùir dhearg,
ged a chaidh a leigeil suas
fad greis

MOUNTAIN ROAD

between a village in the Mountain
and Charlottetown yonder,
from snow above deserts
and snow over seas,
cold enters his bones,
heat comes into her face

and the two of them –
an Ottoman emigrant,
a girl from fishing stock –
eyes
falling on each other

they stop,
and my family's road
appears,
cut through trees and red earth,
though abandoned
a while

A' Bheinn: Mount Lebanon

CAOIDH AN DÈIDH NOLLAIG 2004
(mar chuimhneachan air Ailean 'Òrd' MacNeacail)

is goirid an dèidh
crith-mhara
an eara-dheas,
shiubhail thu
far do chladaich fhèin

is mar bhuaidh fhada
lèirsgrios,
a' sìor dhol am meud,
latha an dèidh latha,
fad seachdain na dhèidh

fhuaradh brath
do bhàis chèin,
ann am post-
dealain, a thug crathadh
air an t-saoghal-sa

mar tsunami
a' bualadh tràigh

BOXING DAY LAMENT 2004
(in memory of Allan 'Òrd' Nicolson)

and shortly after
the tremor
of the south-east sea,
you shoved off
your own shore

and like the after-effects
of utter desolation,
forever increasing,
day after day,
a full week on

notice came
of your distant death
in an e-
mail, that shook
this world

like a tsunami
beating a beach

Lyn Moir

SHORELINE

Out here where blue meets grey meets dove
meets green, and lines of white curls comb
the water's edge

a seagull furls its wings and lands
splay-footed on the endless sands
bladderwrack-fringed,

green necklacing the line between
wet and dry, the map-marked shore
outlined in ink.

I stand, one foot on land one foot
on sea, contrasting hemispheres
trapped underfoot

while you dance over frontier lines
and, holding out your crescent hands,
support the moon.

Jacklin Murray

BELLE'S DISCO – 1982

The evening sun casts shadows on the floor as Belle takes her seat. She is almost demure as she smoothes her skirt, adjusting her hair to conceal the small hearing aid nestling behind her right ear. Now settled, she waits for the dancing to begin.

From the radio on the table before her, Robbie Shepherd begins his introduction of the band for this evening's entertainment. Belle does not quite hear who they are, but catches the name, McLeod. She knew a musician called McLeod once, so this accordionist could be one of the sons. She smiles to herself at the thought of a family continuing, then shivers at the thought of what is to come for her own family, who will not continue in the way they do now.

Her man watches her sitting there, absorbed in the Saturday evening ritual that he will not disturb. His eyes smile softly as he tells her that he will take a turn round the garden and eases himself from the armchair. He is not old, but illness has weakened him. His step as he leaves the room is measured.

Belle does not acknowledge that he has spoken. It is not deliberate: she is deaf and her hearing concentration is focused on the radio.

He does not mind.

Belle is caught up in the breathless rush of the Dashing White Sergeant: set to your partner, spin, turn and move down the hall. The music is loud and fast and she briefly catches the hand of the boy from the British Linen Bank who wanted nothing more than to take her dancing. She would not oblige: there were better dancers on the floor. From the corner of her eye, she sees her man standing in the doorway then spins away for another set.

His lack of interest in the music and the dance is no longer a question between them. That something she loves should not be shared is accepted and does not need to be talked about. They have had long years together but have never danced. He claimed not to see the sense of it and scoffed at the idea of learning. Belle knows him well and thinks it is because he was always too shy and couldn't bear the thought of people looking at him. An unconfessed fear of making a fool of himself.

She has never told him what she thinks about his not dancing.

Robbie is talking to the band leader while the dancers catch their breath. Through the window, Belle watches her man make his slow way around the garden, knowing that she is losing him as, day by day, he diminishes. The weeds are claiming the borders and the grass needs cutting. They should get someone to tidy it up, but she knows he will see this as another defeat.

The Gay Gordons has already started by the time she returns to the hall, which is a pity, as it is one of her favourites. She waits on the sidelines, ready to step in at an appropriate break, and sees their son appear in the garden with his own child in his arms. The little boy squirms to get down and come in the house. The men explain to him that he cannot disturb Granny right now. She knows this because she can lip-read a little. Their son tells the wee lad that Belle's Disco is on the radio and that he must be quiet if he goes in the house.

Belle enjoys the family joke, feeling good that her children keep it going.

The child is set down and makes his unsteady way to the kitchen door. His going leaves their son uncomfortable in the company of his now frail father. The younger man cannot accept that soon there will be an ending and she can do nothing about it: cannot step in at an appropriate moment.

The wee boy appears beside her and climbs onto her knee. They sit out the Eightsome Reel, but Belle taps her foot to the music, making him laugh. He is a good child and sits quietly while Robbie has another chat with the band but, eventually, he tires of stillness, as children do, and wriggles to the floor, tottering off in search of his father.

Her man's tobacco tin, papers and lighter are on the mantelpiece and Belle rises from her seat to fetch them. With deft fingers she fashions herself a smoke and inhales deeply, setting the makings down on the table beside the radio. This is one of the little incongruities that give people cause to hesitate and look at her again. A conventional woman who likes to roll her own. The habit doesn't fit the image.

She doesn't care.

The dancers are lining up for a Military Two Step and she puts the cigarette out in anticipation of the music starting. As she waits, her glance falls on their wedding photograph. He was surprised when she brought it down here and set it on the sideboard, asking her why. She, pretending not to hear, did not answer.

Shrugging his shoulders at her deafness, he had not asked again; but had not removed it either.

They were very young to be marrying, but it was wartime. Who knew whether they would grow old? They both look at the camera, as if to miss the shot would be to miss their life. Belle is wearing a suit, or rather a costume as it was then called, and carries roses from her mother's garden. He, in a naval uniform that does not sit perfectly across the shoulders, looks out guardedly. Belle cannot find another word to describe it: the look of someone who is not at all sure they should be where they are, and are waiting for someone to release them.

Guarded is the best she can do.

Picking up the photograph she studies her man's image. The war was hard on him. When this was taken he had already spent a year on the Arctic Convoys, with four more to do. Even now, his experiences reach out to taint their life.

Today, another war is raging, and she can see him relive his own terrors whenever there is news of a ship going down.

Belle takes the picture back to the table, setting it beside her as the music takes them proudly round the hall.

There is, Robbie tells her, to be a solo performance next while the dancers take another break.

Solo means alone. Soon she will have to come to grips with being alone. The thought creates a frisson of disquiet within her. She has never been alone and does not understand the concept. When he is gone, she thinks, there will be a power struggle among their children. The beginnings of it are showing now. Each will want to claim her for their own. They are her children, she knows them well and he will not be here.

Belle closes her eyes and tries to listen, but hears only – solo.

The programme moves towards its close, with Robbie thanking the band and the dancers, his broad Doric tones wrapping her in a comforting blanket of familiarity. Her man returns, carefully carrying a cup of tea which he sets down in front of her. The flesh of his hands translucent, the bones standing out as he grips the saucer.

Belle's fingers twine briefly over his as she steps up for the last waltz with the shy sailor in the ill-fitting uniform.

Ronnie Nixon

STEWART CHRIST

Stewart Christ went into his local for a glass of wine.
He didn't know that he was Stewart Christ.
He knew himself as Stewart Patrick Delaney.
His true lineage had been disguised by

his

great, great,
great, great,
great, great,
great, great,
great, great,
great, great, great, great, great, great,
great, great, great, great, great, great,
great, great, great, great, great, great,
great, great,
great, great,
great, great,
great, great,
great, great,
great, great,
great, great,
great, great,
great, great,
great, great,
great, great,
great, great,
great, great,

Grandfather.

Who, for appearances' sake, had denied paternity.

THYROID EYES

The doctor told her that she had,
Thyroid eyes.
She took this as a compliment
And went as a frog
To the next fancy dress party in the village.

She came second.

A boy,
With even better thyroid eyes,
Went as Toad
From Toad Hall.

And won the first prize:

Of an all expenses paid
Holiday for two
In a Florida swamp.

ESCALATOR (please get on at the bottom left of page for a safe journey)

except for puzzled eyes,
sank
and with a blank expression,
once
stood stock-still,
more
the fourth step from the top,
from
momentarily,
view.
turned around on what was,

she gave up,

After several attempts,

and kept disappearing from sight.

the final few steps at the top,

she could not manage

Every time she tried,

and she was trying to go up it.

it was the going down escalator

at Glasgow Airport:

attempting to climb up the escalator

of around eleven years of age,

There was a well-built girl,

Vix Parker

MAKING SOUP IN A STORM

She knows when she wakes that it had snowed. Knows it from the muffled light and the silence, knows it with a sinking feeling inside. The entire space of the skylight in her bedroom has filled up with snow, and from a downstairs window she can see the shapes of things outside made huge and indistinct by the sudden fall.

She knows it would be pointless, but she has to try anyway. She puts on boots, scarf, hat, coat, and goes out into the snow. She takes the shovel from the shed and clears a space all around her car, then on down the track that was her driveway, as far as the depression in the white blanket which indicates the lane. The snow reaches to her knees. It takes her an hour and by the time she has finished she is hot and has taken off the coat. From here she can see the short distance to the road where the plough has been through, pushing the snow to one side. She goes back to the car and scrapes all the snow off the windows and the bonnet, but leaves it standing a hand-span high on the roof.

The sky remains heavy and overcast, and as she drives down the cleared track large flat flakes begin to fall thickly. When she reaches the uncleared lane, the wheels of the car begin to lose traction and spin and she has to work the accelerator and clutch gently to ease the car slowly forward. It occurs to her that she should have cleared the lane all the way down. Just before she reaches the ridge of snow pushed aside by the plough, the car begins to slide to the left. It happens so slowly that she has time to think, 'I'm sliding sideways. I should do something about that.' The wheels on the left side sink into the soft earth at the side of the track, and no amount of manoeuvring will get them out again. In fact, the more she tries, the worse they sink. Eventually she gives up, turns off the engine, and gets out. She stands in the road for a moment, looking first one way and then the other (only one side has been cleared and this is being quickly obliterated by the fast-falling snow). She can see no more than fifty metres in either direction. She can no longer see her cottage through the grey curtain.

She takes the warm coat out of her car, puts it on, and

trudges back up the lane. The car, abandoned, sits listing slightly to one side, looking awkward. She leaves footprints in the snow on the path she had so recently cleared.

Once inside she stands for a while, not knowing what to do. She can hear the tick of the clock in the kitchen. The snow which has followed her in and settled on the doormat slowly melts. Eventually she takes off her boots and goes into the kitchen, where she turns on the radio. They are reading out a list of closed schools; her own school is among them. They aren't expecting her in today anyway. She changes the channel and listens to the *Today* programme instead, although she isn't really listening. She makes coffee and toast, but eats only one bite before drifting through to the other room to stand gazing out of the window. The snow continues to fall, wiping everything out. She wonders if she could call someone up at the farm and ask them to bring a tractor and tow her car onto the road.

The sudden sound of the phone ringing startles her. She knows it's her sister before she lifts the receiver. There is a rustling on the line, as though the snow falling between them even muffles their conversation.

'Emma?'

'Yes,' she says. Who else?

'You're not coming, are you.'

'No,' she says, 'I'm not coming.'

'I can't believe it, you won't even come down now, now of all times. I can't believe you.'

She says nothing about the state of the roads, of her car lying abandoned half in a ditch. She doesn't say that she tried. She says nothing.

'Dad needs us here. I can't believe you're making me do this on my own. You're so selfish, Emma, you were always selfish and you've never changed. You'd come if you wanted to, it's not snowing that much.'

'Sorry, Claire,' she says, and puts the phone down gently. Her sister rings back immediately, but she lets it ring on, and after a minute or so it stops.

She lights the fire because it's getting cold and she doesn't want to put the heating on yet. Her cat comes down from the bedroom and curls up in a corner of the sofa. Emma curls in the other corner and tries to read, but she can't concentrate. She takes out some papers she needs to mark, but can't concentrate on these either. She goes upstairs and makes the bed, then cleans the bathroom; something she's been meaning to do for a week. In the kitchen she takes down one of the cookery books that were her mother's and leafs through the soup section. She peels carrots and chops an onion, dissolves a stock cube in boiling water, leaves everything simmering in a pan. While she's doing this the house is buffeted by gusts of wind and the snow flies past the window. At one point she feels a sudden stab of nostalgia that makes her put down the knife and hold on to the edge of the counter until her fingers turn white at the tips. The memory of the day she left home for college comes into her head, unbidden. Her parents drove her to Aberdeen in a car they borrowed from a neighbour, and after they had unloaded her things into the flat she was to share with two other girls, they drove away. She stood on the pavement, watching them go, feeling the unknown freedom of living away from home for the first time ever. Nobody waved. Nobody hugged each other. Nobody cried. She watched the backs of their heads until they were out of sight, knowing that they were really gone, that she was no longer bound to them, that she could be anyone she wanted to be.

When the soup is cooked she puts it in the blender and adds a little cream to it. It looks and smells good, but she eats none of it, instead pouring it into a plastic container to put in the fridge later.

She opens the front door and looks out at the still-falling snow. She can just make out the hump of her car, covered over again. Snow catches in her hair and on her face and the front of her. Her cat comes to stand beside her, sniffing the air, but doesn't venture outside. The phone rings again. It's her father this time.

'Emma.'

'Dad.'

'I suppose there's too much snow.'

'Yes.'

There is a long pause, during which she listens to the indistinct voices from the radio in the kitchen and the hissing of the snow falling on the phone line. She wonders if he's calling from the hospice or from the cream-coloured council house she grew up in. She tries to picture him in either place, but cannot. The cat comes in and sits in front of her, looking into the fire.

'Your mother.'

'Has she ... ?'

'Yes.'

'OK. I'll come down when I can.'

'Right.'

She continues to hold the receiver to her ear even after the click of him hanging up and the hum of the dial tone. She sits and stares into the fire, not really thinking of anything, thinking that she should be thinking of something. There hadn't been much time between when she was diagnosed and now, but it had been enough time for Emma to come to terms with it, and to accept it. She feels as if she'd always known it would happen. She had known it especially since Claire's call last night to say that their mother was in the hospice again. She knows she could have driven down last night and sat beside her mother's bed, but it would have been false and wrong. She knows that nothing would be changed by her death, that none of them would hug each other or cry or miss one another when they weren't there. She knows that she won't visit them any more than she has for the last eight years (which is as little as possible), and that they won't visit her. But something has changed.

Mary Paulson-Ellis

THE STORY OF THE BOY WHO'LL NOT HAVE DONE IT

The boy'll not have done it. He'll be her friend. Her only friend. Sometimes you need a friend. Someone who understands you.

He'll be confused. They'll come at him, nice and slow, nice and friendly like, cups of tea and all, even the offer of an illicit cigarette, treat him like the grown-up they want to make him out to be. He's only fourteen, or so they say on the street. Maybe fifteen. Who knows the truth.

They'll tell him like it is and he will nod. He'll think, You understand me. They'll talk to him of what a lovely girl she was. How bright and smiley. How she loved to tease. They'll say, Think of her mother sitting at home this minute, right now, curtains drawn, bastard press outside her house tapping on her windows. Poor woman.

They'll say, You liked her, didn't you? The nod. Perhaps you even loved her. The nod. How is it that they understand?

They'll say, Her mother loved her too. The nod. Her father. The nod. Her wee brother Callum and Hayley, wee Hayley. She's been crying ever since. Imagine having to grow up without a big sister. You've got a sister, haven't you? The nod. How would you feel if she just disappeared one day? You'd want to know, wouldn't you? The nod.

We understand, son, it was probably an accident. Wanted something, eh? Pushed it a bit far. We know how it is. Young lad like you. It must have been exciting. First girlfriend, eh? Nod, little smile this time on the corner of his lip and the men exchange glances.

Did you kiss her? I bet you wanted to. She was pretty, wasn't she? Lovely hair, smile. I would have if I were your age. It's lonely, son, isn't it? We understand. You need a friend sometimes. Someone special.

The eyes drop to the floor and the men glance at each other again. Behind the glass fingers tighten on folded arms. Just tell us where she is, son. That's all we want to know. Where she's gone. Perhaps you had a row. Perhaps you wanted something and she didn't. Perhaps she was upset. We understand. It can be like that sometimes. Love. And they pause because they see this is the truth, for the boy reaches for his polystyrene cup of tea (milk one sugar – aye, just how I have it, son, you're in good company) and his fingers shake and it slops a little as he pulls it towards him off the table. Behind the glass the officers set their mouths in a line and they sigh. It's looking bad for the boy.

Back inside he's crying now. His mum sitting next to him clenches the shredded tissue in her hand. She's been warned. Best to be quiet. The boy's hand shakes and tea spills on his leg.

It's OK, son. It's OK. We understand.

Tears fall down his cheeks and he doesn't wipe them away, lets them drop onto his jumper and his hand where it sits in his lap holding the tea. And for once the police are silent and they all hold their breath.

And then he speaks.

I didn't mean to.

He means something different. I know he does. She's well gone by now. Gone to her new life. Left it all behind. The boring mum, the ignorant father, the bastard teachers never getting off her back, the stupid girls all souking up one minute and turning nasty the other. She feels bad about him, likes him and all, but he's a bit too serious for her. She doesn't mean to go that far. Just thinks of it like the trip they took the year before. Forgets to get off the bus, that's all. And once you're there, well, it gets hard to go back.

They have him now. The air in the room goes up a notch. The men behind the glass smile with pressed lips and nod to each other and the others look up and at the mirror, sit back in the chairs, their hands flat, their fingers laid out on the edge of the table and wait. A new man comes in and they stand. Hello, son, he says. The boy's mother grips her tissue, her hands together, her eyes wide. So this is how it happens.

We had a row that's all. And the boy is sullen now. Now he has decided. I didn't mean to.

Didn't mean to what, son? says the new man in the room. He sits on the edge of the table.

Didn't mean to shout at her.

You shouted at her?

Yes, we had a row. She was pissed off with me. His mother tightens and the boy casts her a glance. His hands curl closer around the warm cup of tea.

A row, son?

Yes, a row. This time he looks up. The officer crosses his arms.

What about, son?

The boy looks down again. Nothing.

Nothing? Why didn't you want to tell us if it was nothing?

It was just ...

What, son? Just what?

It was stupid.

Stupid? They're not giving him any leeway now. In what way was it stupid?

I don't know, just stupid. I ... He looks at his mother again ... I asked her to marry me.

The men behind the mirror drop their arms to their sides, take a step closer to the glass. To marry you? The man in the room can't hide his surprise. This is not the way it's supposed to go.

The boy's mother drops her hands to her lap and briefly closes her eyes. Her romantic son. Her sensitive boy, always the first to cry. Always without a best friend. Always in search of someone to love him. She'd done her best. On her own. With his little sister too, all bright and out there. And he'd been so quiet, so quiet all these last couple of years. Her first born. She dropped her head in relief. He'd gone daft over a girl, that was all. He'd gone daft over a girl and now he was embarrassed and upset because she was gone and he thinks he's to blame.

The policemen know she's right. They see her look. Her resolve. Behind the glass one man shakes his head and another leaves to go back to his desk. Inside the officer sits and rubs his thumb and finger across his forehead. Tell me, son. It's OK. It's OK to be embarrassed. Just tell us what happened.

So he does.

How he liked her. How they would hang out together after school. How she hated the other girls and he the boys. How they didn't have any other friends. How they went to the place down by the river because there was a bench there you could sit on and it was quiet. How she used to take out her brush and brush her long hair and she would let him do it for her. How they would hold hands and share packets of crisps. Salt and vinegar. How her little fingertips were so pink and almost see-through, like his little sister's used to be when she was a baby. How she would talk about not liking her mum and her dad being stupid. About how she was going to go away and why didn't he come too? But he said he couldn't, what about his mum? And she hadn't mentioned it for a while. And then once, they'd kissed, then laughed. And it was after that he asked her.

She laughed. Then she saw he was serious. And she said, But I can't, I'm going away. And he said, Don't go away. And they rowed. And she stormed off. And he went home. And then when he heard that she was gone he had been frightened. He knew it was all his fault. If only he'd agreed to go with her. Or not said the thing about getting married. He'd put too much pressure on her. He should have left it just the way it was. Friends and everything. And he's crying now. I love her, he says. I love her. And he's the only one who talks as though she's still here.

After that they let him go and he leaves the police station with his mother's arms around his shoulders and his head dipped, eyes to the floor. The police send a woman to sit down with the girl's mother. Where might she have gone? What places would she run to? Do you have relatives, or friends she might stay with? What about your husband? What does he think?

And the mother, who has prepared herself for the worst, discovers that this, this vanishing into thin air, is much, much more terrible.

Julia Rampen

RECYCLING

After the holiday, I recycle newspapers.
Shovelling past days into an iron abyss,
I find pages still chattering of yesterday
as I rewind time on its printed reels.

The world neatly encapsulated in ink;
I fold disasters in half, make them fit.
Tensions in Europe are scrunched and
a president blots in crescendos of rain.

Between a film star draped in dreams
and footballers scoring grainy goals
the child with no flesh tugs my second.
A baby whose cheeks have been stolen

by famine; whose black eyes have learnt,
at one, what I still don't know. How
terrifyingly beautiful those hollows, lips
and pupils perched on masking bone.

June Ritchie

POTS OF GOLD

You complain
that the rain
depresses and restricts you.
But others
see rainbows,
and dream of
splashing in puddles.

Alison Swinfen

MY GARDEN: A POEM IN THREE DAYS

I: Friday

The knocking
had kept me awake
night after night.

Sometimes it was gentle.
Mostly it was
as if my very
heart was the door,
and I trembled lest the wood splinter
under the force.

Life had taught me
to be wary. Perhaps,
with the
pillow over my
head I could
shut out the sound.
And the fear.

Night after night.

And then it stopped.
The knocking. It was no more.
Night after empty night.
Sometimes, in my dreams, I thought
I heard its echo. And I ran to the door
and flung it open, panting, laughing,
eager.

'Here I am.'

But there was no one
in my garden, walking
in the cool of the day.

And the earth, where once
I had sown companion
plants, foxgloves, marigolds
and forget-me-nots,
had been cleared. And in places
there was a dusting
of salt,
where someone
had been crying.

'My garden,'
I screamed,
as the wood splintered.
'What have you done
to my garden?'

That was the first day.

II: Saturday

I knelt, and placed a hand
on the bare earth.
It was white to touch
and felt scented,
with memories of
myrrh.

Slowly I began to press,
kneading
the ground in the hope
it might rise again,
like bread.

Time thudded out its
syncopated rhythm
in heartbeats missed.

And that was the second day.

III: Sunday Breakfast

I stood quite still in
my garden. The rush
over, the heart
steadying into the
serenity of grief.

In the distance
I could see a
small fire blazing
on the beach
and in the air
there was the smell
of a thousand
fish,
cooking.

Men stood around,
tiny, against the dawn,
laughing,
and tearing
at their food, as if
they had been starving for
days.

Not for me the taste
of their fish, or the touch of
warm hands, or the breaking of
bread.

It was the third day, and I began walking,
in the cool of the day.

LIGHT CATCHING

Let us go light catching.
There are places where
there are great
shafts of it,
and nets lie idle
waiting for the
catchers
to come.

Let us go light catching.
Let us cease our angry wrestling
with angels and demons
for a while,
and watch it
play in these places,
low and long.

Let us go light catching,
cabbage white,
meadow blue.
And let us be bright, as
the light flutters by.

For the time for
light harvest
is come and
good work needs
tortoise shell
and painted ladies.

Judith Taylor

HALLOWS

Scooping out the wet flesh from a pumpkin
or a neep, we make an imitation skull
and give it the basics of a face so it can laugh at us.
A soft skull, with a tealight
to impersonate its spirit.

But the light it sheds is warm
and coloured: orange-red, like a torch
seen through fingertips. The flesh colours everything, as the
year declines
– yellow leaves in drifts; berries blackening on the thin trees
until the birds are hungry.

You'd almost think the dead were hungry too,
the way we give them little offerings:

a toy on a grave; silk flowers on a tree beside the road.
Tears and cries
in the public gallery, at a sentence; tears and curses
in a kitchen, when there's nobody there to hear.

They turn away from us. We long for them to remember,
but we couldn't bear to think of ourselves
pleading. And we have made down
the only ceremonial we fell heir to, that would call them,
into a child's game

decorating our house with lit, laughing skulls,
the Day of the Dead. Lucky for us
it fails again. What would we say to our loved dead, if they
and not the neighbours' children came
to rattle our windows?

If we saw them again, matter-of-fact
as green birch in a garland – and their whole selves,
not as we remember – could we endure it if they stayed?

We turn away; in the end it's kind of them
to forget us.

And winter comes, again: the trees are stripped bare,
and the lanterns grin, blackening, from the midden.
They leave a ghost of their own
lingering, cornered, in our lit house:
the odour of new decay.

Chiew Siah Tei

A SLICE OF THE MID-AUTUMN MOON

Spring, and it's the first day of Mingzhi's schooling.

The six-year-old walks through the paddy fields, escorted by his family butler. There is occasional chirping of crickets from the bushes along the path, and cheeping of birds on the branches above. Mingzhi glances here and there, trying to figure out where they are, the crickets and birds. He manages to spot a couple of birds and cheers, hearing his voice echo in the wideness. He giggles, staring up at his butler. The stout man remains silent, his face expressionless. Mingzhi finds another bird, a cricket and a couple of dragonflies. More cheers, more echoes, more giggles. And the same silence from his butler. No sooner, Mingzhi gives up with his game. He keeps walking. He knows he has to walk past the bridge and enter the village where the school is located. The bridge is not very far away, he notices, yet still, the route seems too long, too quiet.

'Why can't Eldest Sister come with me?' He asks.

The butler does not answer.

Mingzhi begins to recite from *Sanzi Jing*, remembering the lines as taught by his uncle.

'Human beings are born with the same kind nature;
Their learning process later sets them apart ...'

It will be wonderful if Sister Meilian and Meifong can be there reciting with me at the school. Imagining he and his sisters sitting together in the classroom, reading the lines, Mingzhi gets excited and raises his voice, only to be hushed up by the butler.

'We are almost there, Eldest Grand Young Master. Please behave yourself.'

After school Mingzhi rushes home, can't wait to be his sisters' teacher. He smoothes rice paper on his study desk and demonstrates his calligraphy skills.

Fourteen-year-old Meilian and five-year-old Meifong crowd forward.

'Let's begin from the basics.' He lowers his voice, touches

his chin, mimicking his teacher who always smoothes his whiskery white beard.

His sisters giggle. Meifong, the youngest, pats her brother's head. Mingzhi laughs, dodging. He writes, starting with a right falling stroke, joined by a left one from the middle of the first stroke. Black ink seeps through the rice paper. The strokes stand up: two legs supporting the body. *Ren*, 'human'. The girls study the strokes, trying to associate the character with that pronunciation in their daily conversation.

Then they rush after Mingzhi's brush. He hides it behind him.

'Not yet.'

Mingzhi adds a line horizontally across the first stroke. That gives *da*, 'big': a man with both his arms stretching out wide.

'One more.'

He swiftly presses a dot in between the strokes, turning it into *tai*, 'greatest'.

The girls observe the changes. *Like magic.*

Ren – Da – Tai.

They read aloud after their brother.

Taking their turns, they hold the brush for the first time. Though her hands tremble, Meilian, the eldest, manages to copy the strokes. Her lines are thin and shaky.

'Like chicken claws,' teases Meifong.

But she is not much better, both the legs of her 'human' jumble to the left. And she is fond of dots, making hundreds of them on the paper.

'Stop it, what a waste!'

Meilian reaches for the brush. Meifong dodges her, runs brandishing the brush, splashing the black ink about the room, onto her sister and her brother. *Too much.* They cup a handful of ink each and chase after Meifong.

Their first lesson ends with the three black faces laughing at each other, before the asthmatic Meifong flops into a chair, coughing breathlessly. Mingzhi watches as Meilian smoothes Meifong's chest, until her breathing eases. Mingzhi stares at the two smeared faces in front of him, almost unrecognisable. Like strangers. A sudden fear rushes over him. *My sisters! I want my sisters! I want to see their smiles!* Panicked, he hurries for a moist cloth and rubs his sisters' faces with it – despite them screaming, protesting his act – until the ink is wiped away, and he looks at them, their clean, pinkish cheeks, and feels safe.

In the following days, his eldest sister Meilian waits for him to come home in the afternoons and asks him his lessons for the day. The sister and brother hide in Mingzhi's room. Meilian listens to Mingzhi reciting poems, telling tales as told by his teacher, explaining the teachings of Confucianism.

Mingzhi notices that his eldest sister learns as fast as he does. By dusk before dinner she recites the poems together with him, and is able to explain the metaphor behind those that are too difficult for a six-year-old: the solitude, the feelings of loss or resentment nicely wrapped under beautiful landscapes: the vast snowy land, the magnificent gorges, the borderless steppe, the roaring Yellow River or the quiet Yangzi Jiang. Mingzhi likes listening to his eldest sister, her voice soft and comforting. He lays his head on her lap, his cheek against the smoothness of her silk dress.

At night, lying in his bed Mingzhi stares hard at the light beams silting through the seams of the planked wall, listening to his eldest sister's whispers from the next-door, vague, indistinct. Imagining her telling her younger sister at her bedside the story she had learned; imagining Meifong falling asleep before it ends.

Sometimes after the lights are put out, he hears his eldest sister reciting the poems by her favourite poet, Li Qingzhao, the greatest woman poet of the Song Dynasty. Mingzhi remembers Meilian once told him about the miserable life Li had led, about her marriage, the war and her second marriage. What is marriage? What is war? Why did she have to marry again? He doesn't understand. And her sister would keep quiet whenever he asked her the questions. He thinks she doesn't understand, too.

But most of the time, Mingzhi falls asleep before his sister stops reciting. There is always a herd of sheep walking into his dream, dotted on the vast, green steppe of Mongolia, exactly the way his eldest sister described it when they read the poems.

'It's beautiful, Eldest Sister,' he would murmur and roll over, falling deep into his dreamland.

Summer, and Mingzhi is not allowed to return to the school. He feels the strange atmosphere at home. At first the servants gather in groups, whispering amongst themselves; their faces are pale and their lips tremble. And then some of them disappear one after another, returning a few days later in their bulgy red eyes, from which tears quietly stream.

'There's been a plague.' His eldest sister pulls him aside, trying to explain. She says it started with the cattle: pigs, cows, oxen, chicken, ducks die with their mouths spewing out foaming spittle and their bellies protruding; then the weakest among the children.

'Where do the pigs and cows and oxen and chicken and ducks and the children go to when they die?' Mingzhi asks his eldest sister. Meilian scratches her head and then shrugs her shoulder.

Mingzhi misses his school. He misses writing and reading and reciting. *I can set up a school at home!* He gets his ink and brush and rice paper ready in his room, waiting for his sisters to join him. He waits, and waits, but there is no sign of them. Mingzhi rushes to his sisters' room and is surprised to see a crowd in it. He squeezes in and finds his younger sister Meifong lying unconscious in bed, his mother sitting by her side, rubbing her body with a wet cloth. Meifong vomits occasionally. Her face is as red as an over-ripe persimmon.

Mingzhi finds his eldest sister in a corner. He holds her hand tight, standing aside with her, watching their mother hold Meifong's jaw open, forcing herbal medicine into her mouth. Excess liquid flows along the corners of Meifong's lips, staining the pillow, spreading instantly, black against the white sheet. Mingzhi feels weak; his hand squeezes Meilian's fingers. She lets him, does not yell.

By evening Mingzhi sees that foaming spittle start spewing from Meifong's mouth. His mother asks Meilian to take him to his room, and sends a maid to their grandfather, asking that a doctor be sent for.

The grandfather says nothing.

Late at night Mingzhi hears his mother's cry, long and tearing. The brother and sister cling tight together in bed and weep under the blanket.

Come autumn, Mingzhi's grandfather falls ill on the evening

of the Moon Festival. The garden dinner for the family is cancelled.

In the courtyard, Mingzhi watches as his eldest sister hangs a lantern on the branch and says it's for Meifong. They stand in silence. Moments later Meilian beckons him, preparing to lead a lantern parade around the courtyard. Candlelight, thin and soft, flickers in the colourful paper stripes. The wind is strong, clears the cloud and shakes their lanterns. They bring the fragile lanterns close to their bodies and shield the candles with their hands. Their eyes glow, reflecting the light, and their faces shine, colourful.

Before the first round ends Mingzhi shouts, 'Let me take the lead!'

As he rushes forward Mingzhi stumbles over a stump and falls. His face is pressed into a pool of mud and his paper lantern burns off in seconds. Meilian laughs out loud. *Finally, she smiles again.* Mingzhi laughs, too, and he tugs at Meilian's sleeves, pulling her onto the ground. The sister and brother sit in the muddy pool and giggle. Looking up, Mingzhi sees his eldest sister's smiling face clean and bright, like the moon above her.

Mingzhi doesn't know his happiness has infuriated his grandfather. In his room, the old man lies awake in bed; his head aches as he listens to the children's laughter. He thinks about the inauspicious death of the young girl. And now, his own illness.

From the courtyard, Meilian's laughter seems to be irritating.

Girls, useless.

Outside, Mingzhi keeps laughing as he wrestles with his sister, not knowing that his grandfather has made a decision that will change their lives.

Meilian's wedding is scheduled for the following month: to drive away all evils and restore good fortune. Mingzhi's grandfather happily announces the bridegroom-to-be: the eldest son of the district mandarin, thirty-eight years old; and Meilian is to be his second wife.

Meilian stops coming to Mingzhi's room, and keeps herself to hers.

Mingzhi asks his mother, 'What does "getting married" mean? Is Eldest Sister leaving us forever?'

His mother pats his head and sighs. There is a long silence.

'You will know later, son, you will know.'

On the wedding day Mingzhi sees his eldest sister being led into the red-curtained sedan. The autumn wind slaps her ferociously and the silk gown clings tight to her body, lean and tremulous. Mingzhi can't see Meilian's face under her red headscarf, but remembers her look under the autumn moonlight. Smiling, clean and bright.

And the sedan takes her away.

Fiona Ritchie Walker

SADIE WRITES A NOTE

(In 1907, an advertising campaign offered free cereal to every woman who would wink at her grocer.)

Wanting to be well-presented,
I thought to save on my housekeeping
and use money meant for cereal
to buy myself some rouge.

Not wishing to offend Mr Diamond,
I visited the grocer two blocks down,
after staring into the bathroom mirror
deciding which eye to use.

I did not know it was his first day
and being unaware of the advertisement in question,
he thought me about to faint,
so carried me to a chair.

I did not buy the rouge. He says
he likes the natural bloom on my cheeks
and we needed all our money
to buy the railcar tickets.

Please water the pot plants on Mondays
and pay the window cleaner.
You will see I have left you
six packs of Battle Creek Toasted Corn.

Jane Webster

THE WOMAN IN THE MIRROR

She has long dark hair parted in the middle and trying to hide the boniness of her face and shoulders. There are shadows under her eyes, certainly, but nothing too dramatic. No bruises, no sediment of mascara left after the ebb of tears. I can detect a thinning in the skin on her neck, but there are no claw marks, no serrated lines to cut along. She keeps her secrets well, the woman in the mirror.

I turn and leave her, conscious that she continues to watch me, I suspect with pity. She has a face made for reflection and consideration. You could never imagine such a woman in the throes of sexual abandonment, or see her well-spaced eyes slanting with possessiveness. I close the door on her and lock it on emptiness.

If this is shock, it seems oddly similar to my normal state. The school hasn't changed, the Monday morning adolescents wheeling and squawking in the playground, vicious as herring gulls rummaging scandal. I float between them like a glass bottle holding a message nobody wants. As I drift to my classroom colleagues address me and I answer politely, and even smile, remembering afterwards to take it off my face and save it for later.

The day is just like any other. The school lurches from one bell to the next, an education omnibus, while the students stare out the windows and occasionally read. At the end of the day they run away screaming, and I follow slowly after them, cradling homework to be corrected. When I get back she's waiting for me, hiding upstairs, reluctant to remind me of our reality. I make coffee and mark essays, light lamps and close the curtains so the woman can't inadvertently stare at me. I switch the television on but do not watch it. It carries on a conversation with itself, happily self-absorbed, while I move from one room to another, looking for something I've lost.

She is very sorry, the woman in the mirror. She has the utmost sympathy for me. I look at the tears brimming in her eyes and hate them. She flinches, and I know she would vanish if she could.

Nights are longer than days. Nights are unpleasant. They begin by murdering the sun, smothering it in its own blood-drenched pillows. Then they sneak into town, sheltering pain and despair under their cloak of shadows. They wait at the edge of the lamplight, dark eyes avid for death and deconstruction. A quick, clean death is never enough for them. Nights thrive on terror, on eyes staring sightlessly and lips cracking on pitiful pleas to a dementing God. Nights are very unpleasant indeed, and much too long in Scotland. Unless you're a lover.

On lovers, night cheats. It backs off, smiling, while a hand touches a face and traces the line of neck and shoulder. It swirls darkness and light into a maelstrom while one body arcs into another and limbs pull each other ever closer into the crescendo of wave breaking upon wave, listens in glee to cries sweet and plaintive as skimming terns. Then, in pure vindictiveness, it sets stars to watch over them and shimmer in their sweat. Night knows what follows in love's wake, and waits to gorge.

The woman in the mirror holds no truck with night.

The practicalities of separation I deal with easily. The mortgage was small, and my salary easily assimilates his half. Life's much cheaper alone. Cooking and eating are quicker. On Friday night I still buy a bottle of wine and drink all of it, rather than a third. The room reels and even night is too fastidious to watch me retching.

Saturday dawns like a taunt. I wake with the first blackbird reiterating his small stubborn spell, and through the gap in the badly closed curtains I watch the sky changing colour like a bruise in reverse. When I hear the newsagent creaking open his shutters I get up and pack my rucksack, and flee the village.

Even so day beats me to it. She dances in reunion with the hills, catching up first a slope of bracken red as a fox, then a stream more brilliant than diamonds. Me she greets politely, not really wanting to wait for my slow footsteps. I lace on my hill boots and follow her.

Hillwalking is a highly suitable occupation for a middle-aged Scottish teacher of English. My body, at least, is faithful and easily falls back into rhythm, though my stomach reminds me that I haven't fed it for some considerable time. Tonight, I promise it, we'll eat. Beans on toast or cheese. Tonight will be all right again. I scramble up the steep rocks of the Law, plough steadily upwards at forty-five degrees. Around me the Forth Valley starts to fall into perspective, and at the rock called Lookaboutye I do just that, my body mimicking the savagery of orgasm, my breath in shallow gasps and my T-shirt sticking to me. The river now shows its serpentines, furrowing in and out of the land like lovers pursuing each other's secrets. I turn my back on them and climb into the morning.

In the Ochils you can walk all day, moving from one ridge to another while Scotland unfurls at your feet like a story written in opals. I plunge uphill and down, my legs never faltering, till the light whispers a warning and I head back reluctantly, my feet slowing as I struggle for balance on the steep slopes of the Law. Before the last crag I pause, wondering what there is to go back to.

Once there was a girl who wrote poems and jumped a red roan pony. I see her falling away from me, her face contorted in terror, her thin limbs flailing till at last they come to rest, disjointed and useless as a discarded plastic doll. Cautiously, I scramble down after her and walk away from her corpse, a gaunt and charmless ghost.

In the glen there are rowanberries in profusion, bursting like blood blisters. I note that the winter will be hard.

Back at the house I go through the rituals to disarm night. I force myself to open a can of soup and eat it with bread and butter. I bathe in hot water with herbs added, and try not to listen to the silent creeping of the house. With a warm soft towel I dry myself, tending my unwanted body rather than caring for it. Slipping under the downie, I send out an urgent SOS to Morpheus. Unfortunately, he doesn't get it, and snoozes while night has its way with me.

I feel for you, says the night. No, really I do. I know exactly what you're going through because I know exactly what they're doing, right this minute now. Shall I show you? Do you want to hear the words he whispers to her, feel the silken plumpness of her breast under his hand? Do you want to know his triumph as her young body splits under ...

I sit up and throw a pillow at night. No. I will not have this. Being deserted is quite bad enough, without becoming jealous and embittered. Let him go. Leave me in peace. Ha, sneers night. That was always your answer, wasn't it? Too casual, too quiet, too self-sufficient. No wonder he went. The real wonder is that you were too blind, too trusting to notice what was going on under your own nose. I mean, she was one of your pupils, wasn't she?

I'd taught her for Higher English two years ago. Blonde, keen on drama, not backwards at coming forwards. Rather plump, I'd always thought.

Night snorts and makes comments about women whose hipbones stick out more than their nipples.

And him, whispers night. This man you knew so well. More than twice her age, isn't he? One of his university students, isn't she? A man of integrity, this husband of yours? So sorry and doesn't know how he can do this to you, but all the same he's doing it and leaving you to pay the bills? You wasted twenty years of your life on that?

I try desperately to twist away from night and only tie myself up in the downie. No, I protest, there was something of value there, something between us that was better than both of us. Like an old woman I rummage through the memories of my marriage. The first time I saw him watching me. The first kiss. The first night. His arms around me when my mother died. The feline grace of him as a young man, and the feel of his skin, warm and cool as candlelight. Deliberately, I paper the blackness with images of him.

So touching, says the night. Pity that none of them fit.

On Sunday the woman in the mirror lectures me severely. With cool compassion she advises me that this will not do. We start here, she tells me. What's done is done and gone. We start with this moment, this breath. There. Breathe deeply. Live your life alone. Do what you've always wanted to do.

I stare blankly at her, and her eyelashes twitch in exasperation.

Do something while you're waiting to remember your dreams, then. Take an evening class. That's what all bored single middle-aged women do. And for God's sake do one that gives you at least three hours' homework a night, preferably not wine tasting.

I find the college brochure in the school library and bring it home with me on Monday night. The range of courses is amazing, everything from aromatherapy to Zen via mathematics (applied). One nudges at me, though, and I find myself musing. Gaelic. Scotland's hidden language. How many times have I said I wish I knew it? It must be in me somewhere, whispering in my bloodstream. The language of the boulder on the hillside, a spray of birch leaves flickering gold against a winter sky. I sign up immediately and spend the rest of the evening with the Munro book, flicking through mountain names. *Eididh Nan Clach Geala*, web of the white stones. *Beinn Alligin*, jewelled hill. My mind seeds with possibilities, one of which might sprout into a tendril of happiness.

How he would laugh, says the night, if he knew. Or cared.

The first evening class is cold, fluorescent lit. There are eleven of us, five couples and me, and we huddle in the back row of the classroom. We all wear fleeces and jeans, and quickly establish that we have some connection with walking or climbing. Our teacher has to interrupt a discussion on the Cobbler. He is a stocky man called Tormud, which translates into English as Norman. He greets us with something incomprehensible and we glance at each other. He takes a roll call, ascribing Gaelic names to those that translate and I become Seonaid. Primers are handed out, and we produce A4 pads and ballpoints, start scribing our first tentative phrases: *Ciamar a tha sibh? Tha gu math, tapadh leibh.*

It is an impossible language, skipping away from me like a wagtail on stones in a stream. If it had a verb for have, it would have rules, but not as other languages know them. Nonetheless I persevere, writing fatuous phrases again and again while the rest of the class are more probably sensibly watching *EastEnders.* It gives me something to do, and night does not speak Gaelic.

I haven't quite got round to telling anybody that he's left me. My address is still the same, so it's none of the school's business. With the friends I occasionally go hillwalking with I've never been prone to discussing him. So I continue to keep his secrets, loyal past reason, that reason being I could not cope with their pity. Night's is quite bad enough.

Gaelic makes things easier. There I can speak the bald truth, sheltered by anonymity and lack of vocabulary. *Tha na duine agam. Tha na parantan agam. Tha na clann agam.* Ignorance shelters me from loss.

Our numbers decline steadily, one couple failing to return every fortnight or so. I do not think they have been lost on the hill. Tormud takes this stoically, without comment. Between classes I work hard, ignoring night's asides about middle-aged women desperate for male approval of any sort. I tell myself that by next summer I'll be touring the West Coast, island hopping maybe, able to speak the language of clean waves breaking on white sand while seals sing. Nights are non-existent in the north in summer.

Meanwhile December is upon me and the nights grow longer, with talons of ice. I have to shelter my tendrils of hope, fearing that in this language I'll never grow beyond the niggardliness of buying bread and milk and commenting on the weather. I want the tale of Deirdre and Noisu in Glen Etive, not the stilted politeness of tearoom chatter. Night whispers that I get what I deserve.

Not long before Christmas, I receive a letter from a lawyer. He advises me that my husband would like to buy my half of the house. The alternative is that the house is sold and the profits split.

I remember us buying this house together, ten years ago. I remember the excitement, the phone calls back and forth. I remember moving in and the heating not working, sitting cuddled up together and drinking red wine among the tea chests and cardboard boxes. The dust and the giggles of the do-it-yourself attempts. The argument of espaliered trees versus rambling roses. I remember far too much.

I wonder how he intended to explain all that when he moved her in, and night takes great delight in telling me.

The very next day is the very last Gaelic class. Tormud is stoical still as he explains that the college cannot continue a course that only three people attend. We will, of course, be given a refund. Nodding our understanding, we all make a total hash of negative imperatives.

At the end of the class the last couple invite Tormud and I for a drink. We go to a crowded pub and I sit beside Tormud, sipping thin sour wine and suddenly conscious of the warmth of his body. Christmas plans are discussed; the couple are going to Assynt, staying in a caravan near Lochinver. Tormud is visiting his parents in Lewis. I volunteer nothing, but when the other couple leave I become quite vocal, questioning Tormud about the difficulties of keeping Gaelic alive, his upbringing in Lewis, anything so he doesn't go and leave me alone. After the second glass of wine I manage, *De tha thu ag iarraidh ri cofaidh*, my eyes demurely downcast.

The woman in the mirror averts her eyes hastily as Tormud stolidly climbs the stairs behind me. I'm too busy dealing with night and Tormud to have any time for her. We manage the preliminaries somehow, though I have to remind him that condoms work more effectively on the penis than as a good luck charm left on the bedside table. As he approaches his ponderous climax he croons to me in Gaelic. He could be telling me my skin holds the light of a thousand stars, or that my hair falls over my body like a waterfall at midnight. He could be telling me has acid indigestion and could I kindly get him a Rennie, for all I know, or care.

While he snores I lie awake, feeling my own fluids congealing on my thighs in sterile futility. Night treats my behaviour with the contempt it deserves.

In the morning I bound out of bed and into the bathroom, taking care to make as much noise as possible. Under the shower I scrub my body red as shame, then brush my teeth till the gums bleed. I bundle my wet hair into a turban of towel, bind myself tightly into a shapeless dressing gown.

He's not stupid. He's already in the kitchen, fully dressed and hesitant. When I offer him coffee it's instant, and not in Gaelic. I watch his Adam's apple move as he gulps it down, my eyes as kind as a ferret watching a rat. Something squeezes its fingers round my heart, and I long to tell him that I'm sorry that he was the wrong man in the wrong place at the wrong time. I'm sorry that we'll never get past *ciamar a tha sibh*, because I'm completely unable to interpret his response. I say nothing though, other than a brittle goodbye, and avert my face when he attempts to kiss my cheek.

After he's gone I confront the woman in the mirror. She stares boldly back at me, all innocence. Unsoftened by her hair, I note the intersecting circles that make her face, and reflect that this is the composition of a whore, and a fool. She looks saddened. How can it be? she breathes. I am no more these things than I am unwanted memories, waiting to be packed into a black bag and discarded. I take a step towards her and her eyes widen, showing a paring of bluish white between the brown iris and the eyelid. No, wait! she exclaims. I can explain everything; really I can, if you just give me time.

She is a liar, that woman in the mirror.

TO PIER PAOLO PASOLINI

... the further a poet goes in his development, the greater – unintentionally – his demands on an audience, and the narrower that audience is. The situation oftentimes ends with the reader becoming the author's projection, which scarcely coincides with any living creature at all. In those instances, the poet directly addresses either the angels ... or another poet – especially one who is dead ...

JOSEPH BRODSKY

I

In this country, for which I have no love,
at times it's only when I'm on the train
that I can put together half an hour
for my own thoughts, or find a passage in
a book I bought eleven years ago.
That was how I came across the letter
you had written after you were banished
from that far-off place you loved so much
in the north-east of your country to
begin a new life in the capital.

II

That beloved place was your protection
in the last days of the war when you
had fled the army that had been interned.
You wrapped yourself in its revived language
and wore it like a splendid garment that
you could appear in knowing that it would
make you look stunning each and every time.
Wasn't that your dream, the resurrection
of the neglected Romance languages?
You ransacked the language of the Rhône,

III

the land of Mistral, and across the mountains
on the Spanish border, where the savage
assault of the star and crescent faltered.
You were seeking words and images

Christopher Whyte

DO PIER PAOLO PASOLINI

... the further a poet goes in his development, the greater – unintentionally – his demands on an audience, and the narrower that audience is. The situation oftentimes ends with the reader becoming the author's projection, which scarcely coincides with any living creature at all. In those instances, the poet directly addresses either the angels ... or another poet – especially one who is dead ...

JOSEPH BRODSKY

I

San dùthaich seo, nach eil gaol agam oirre,
aig amannan 's ann air an trèan a-mhàin
nach fhairtlich orm leth-uair a chur ri chèile
airson mo smuaintean fhìn, no airson earrann
a shireadh ann an leabhar ceannaichte
aon bliadhna deug air ais. B' ann air an dòigh
sin a thachair litir rium a sgrìobh thu
an dèidh dhut a bhith fuadaichte bho cheàrn
chèin, ghràdhaichte ann an ear-thuath do dhùthcha,
is beatha ùr a thòiseachadh san Ròimh.

II

Bha i air a bhith 'na teàrmann dhut,
a' cheàrn sin ghràdhaichte, fad lathannan
deireannach a' chogaidh, nuair a theich thu
bho armailt cuirt' an sàs. Rinn thu do phasgadh
'na cainnt ath-nuadhaichte mar gum b' e aodach
gasd' a bh' innte, anns am b' urrainn dhut
do nochdadh, 's tu ro spàideil, anns gach àite.
Nach sin a bha 'na bhruadar dhut, aiseirigh
nan cànan dearmaidte nuadh-Làidinneach,
's tu rannsachadh mu inbhirean an Rhône,

III

an tìr Mhistral, air neo taobh eile bheanntan
iomallach na Spàinne, far na chaisgeadh
ionnsaigh gharg an leth-chearcaill 's an rèil!
Bha thu ag iarraidh fhaclan, ìomhaighean

that you could put to use ennobling
the language that you'd hear upon the lips
of the old women and young lads you met
in the place where your mother grew up.
Your intention was to work in such
a way that they'd have no reason to envy

IV

the great and good in court and parliament
and the polished language that they used.
(I'm interrupted by a voice I know,
a certain woman saying crabbitly,
'This isn't verse you're writing, this is prose,'
complaining that my poems are forever
growing longer, always stretching out,
exhausting her with their verbosity.
Her opinion is that poems should
grow thinner and dilute in every case,

V

as happens in the poems that she writes.
She carves and trims away at them 'til all
that's left upon the naked, hungry sheet
are paltry scraps or even, sometimes, nothing.
It isn't worth her while, wasting her time
eavesdropping on the words I mean for you.
The listening of the dead is ever patient
and you'll have time enough, I'm sure, for all
the things I have to say to you today,
whatever language I decide to use,

VI

even one you never knew existed;
because the kingdom of the dead is the
kingdom of every language and you will
understand me in one way or another.)
They would have excused you if you'd been
a priest, but you had read the work of Marx,

a b' urrainn dhut a chleachdadh gus a' chànain
uaisleachadh, a chluinneadh tu air bilean
nan caillich is nam fiùran òg sa chlachan
far an d' fhuair do mhàthair chaomh a h-àrach.
B' e sin do rùn-sa, obrachadh air dòigh
's nach fhàgte aca cion-fàth de aon sheòrs'

IV

farmad a ghabhail ri cainnt lìomhaichte
luchd sìobhalta nam pàrlamaid 's nan cùirt.
(An-dràsta ruigidh mi uair eile guth
boireannaich àraidh, 'g ràdh gu h-aimhreiteach
gur rosg, 's nach bàrdachd idir, tha mi sgrìobhadh,
a' gearan mar a bhios gach dàn a th' agam
a' dol am faide 's a' sgaoileadh a-mach,
ga claoidheadh leis cho fadalach 's a tha e.
A rèir a beachd-se, cha bu chòir do dhàn
ach dìreach tanachadh is fàs nas caoil,'

V

mar a thachras don a' chuid a th' aice,
i gan snaigheadh is gan snasachadh
gus nach fhàgar air a' phàipear bhochd
ach mìrean sgapt' air neo, uaireannan, càil.
Chan fhiach leatha, co-dhiù, a h-ùine chaitheamh
a' dèanamh farchluais air na their mi riut.
Is dìreach foighidneach claistneachd nam marbh,
is bidh gu leòr a thìde agad, tha
mi creidsinn, airson na th' agam ri ràdh,
ge b' e a' chainnt a chleachdas mi, ge b' e

VI

cainnt nach robh fhios agads' air a bith!
Oir 's i rìoghachd nam marbh rìoghachd gach cainnt,
is faodaidh tu mo thuigsinn air gach dòigh.)
Bhitheadh iad air do shàbhaladh, gun teagamh,
nan robh thu air a bhith 'nad shagart. Ach
rinn thu an fheallsanachd aig Marx a nochdadh,

though educated in a Fascist state,
where, at the decree of the great Leader,
the count of the years had begun again.
You were a communist, not just a poet,

VII

and were wholly rejected on both sides.
For some you suffered from the sickness of
a decadent, perverted bourgeoisie,
for others, overthrew the laws of God.
I was myself in that same village once,
Casarsa, which they call 'the delightful'.
I was going north by train across
the mountains, 'til I reached the place where they
speak only German. We stopped for a while
in darkness and I read the name upon

VIII

the railway sign. I heard no voice, saw no one,
and five years had gone by since you were killed.
It wasn't only language that you found
upon the lips of a young lad you loved,
but the lips themselves, the countenance,
the bodies you saw swimming naked in
that region's shallow, lazy rivers, or
lying on the shingle having stripped
beneath the branches of the trembling trees
that march across that flat land ceaselessly.

IX

You used to love to play football, to dance
at every festival held in the country,
you used to dearly love the innocent
diversions that the young people enjoyed,
and others that were far from innocent.
Someone or other told his mother,
his mother told the priest, and the priest
told the appropriate authorities.

ged a chaidh d' fhoghlam ann an stàit nam pasgan,
's cunntas nam bliadhnaichean air tòiseachadh
a-rithist, a rèir òrdugh a' chinn-fheadhna.
Làmh ri 'nad bhàrd, bha thu 'nad cho-mhaoineach,

VII

is chaidh do dhiùltadh buileach air dà thaobh.
Airson feadhna bha thu tinn le galar
bùirdeasachd chlaointe, is airson feadhn' eil'
chuir thu laghannan Dè bun-os-cionn.
Bha mise fhìn sa chlachan sin aon uair,
Casarsa, ris an canadh iad 'nan aoibhneas',
air trèan a bha siubhal mu thuath, tarsainn
nam beanntan, gu ruig tìr 's nach bruidhnear ach
a' Ghearmailteis. Stad sinn san dorchadas
car sealain, 's leugh mi ainm a' bhaile sgrìobht'

VIII

air clàr. Cha chluinnte guth, chan fhaicte neach,
is mharbhadh tu còig bliadhna roimhe sin.
Cha b' e a' chainnt a-mhàin a nochdadh tu
air bilean fiùrain òig a bha 'na h-adhbhar
gaoil dhut, ach na bilean fhèin, a ghnùis,
na cuirp a chunnaic thu lomnochd a' snàmh
ann an aibhnichean tana, leisg na dùthcha,
no sìnte air a mhol, 's iad air an rùsgadh
fo sgàil nan critheann ioma-ghluasadach
a nì am màrsail sìorraidh trid a' chòmhnaird.

IX

B' ionmhainn leat ball-coise, a bhith dannsa
aig gach uile fhèill a chùimt' san dùthaich,
b' ionmhainn leat gu lèir gach fearas-chuideachd
neochiontach bhios aig na daoine òga,
's cuid eile nach eil idir neochiontach.
Bha feareigin a' bruidhinn ri a mhàthair,
a mhàthair ris an t-sagart, is an sagart
ris na h-ùghdarrasan freagarrach.

When finally the matter came to court
you were cleared of every accusation,

X

but you had left Friuli already.
You could not carry on with your work as
a teacher nor earn anything because
you were a pariah, a laughing-stock.
You were made welcome by the capital,
which was to be your second Casarsa,
Rome, the city where you found new lips,
new words that you would weave together in
a cloth that cried out of your love, a love
that elevated every humble thing.

XI

I was on the train going between
the different places where I work and live,
between Glasgow and Edinburgh with
the abject sun's few rays darting across
the pages of the book sat on my lap;
I came across your words about the room
that you got beside the Jewish ghetto,
not far from the baker's where they still
bake those special, funny little cakes
that I would buy when I was there myself.

XII

Your mother chose to become an exile
and follow you, her son, to the city.
To earn a little money she looked after
the children of a wealthy family,
and stayed with them not far from your own room.
According to the letter you wrote to
the woman friend who was closest to you
and whom you might have married if you'd had
different desires, your inclination
was something you thought separate from yourself,

Nuair a thàinig a' chùis, aig a' cheann thall,
gu ruig taigh-cùirte, bha thu fuasgailte,

X
ach bha thu cheana air an dùthaich fhàgail.
Cha b' urrainn dhutsa leantainn ort ag obair
'nad fhear-teagaisg, no dad a chosnadh, oir
dh'fhàs thu 'nad chùis-dèisinn, 'nad chùis-bhùirt.
Rinn an ceanna-bhaile d' fhàilteachadh
an uair sin, 's e gu bhith 'na Chasars' eile
dhut, an Ròimh, san d' fhuair thu bilean ùra,
faclan ùr' a dh'fhigheadh tu ri chèile
'nan clò a bha 'na èigheachd air do ghaol,
's air mar a dh'uaislich e gach rud bha ìosal.

XI
Bha mi air an trèan, 's i siubhal eadar
m' àite-còmhnaidh 's m' àite-obrachaidh,
eadar Dùn Èideann 's Glaschu, air mo ghlùinean
leabhar fosgailt', gathan gann na grèine
dìblidh a' dol thairis air an duilleig,
is thachair rium na sgrìobhadh leat mun t-seòmar
a fhuair thu faisg air coimhearsnachd nan Iùdhach,
chan fhad' bho bhùth an fhuineadair, san reicear
fhathast cèicean sònraichte is èibhinn
a cheannaichinn fhìn nuair a bha mi ann.

XII
Roghnaich i an fhògarrachd, do mhàthair,
's a mac a leantainn chun a' bhaile mhòir.
Gus beagan a dh'airgead a chosnadh, bha i
frithealadh ri pàisdean teaghlaich bheairtich,
's a' fuireachd anns an taigh aca, chan fhada
bhod sheòmair fhèin. A rèir na sgrìobh thu gus
a' bhanacharaid a bu dlùithe dhut,
a phòsadh tu, is dòcha, nam biodh mianntan
diofaraichte agad, chunnaic thu
'nad chlaonadh rud nach robh a' buntainn dhut,

XIII

a foe forever walking at your side.
Your world had been demolished, all the things
you used to love, the folk, the place, the language,
that was your opinion. All your work
was left without any meaning, sense
or hope of living on. But you were wrong!
That's what I would want to shout if I
was at your shoulder reading; I would reach
across and snatch the pen out of your hand,
to make it clear that your work hadn't finished

XIV

but was just beginning, that you had
not been assigned a place out on the edge
but in the very centre, your perversion,
as you called it, was not a hindrance
to your work but helped it come to fruit.
Though you can hear me now, perhaps, my voice
won't travel far enough to reach you there
in the middle of your disappointment.
But if you are sensitive to every
kind of whisper, however faint it is,

XV

which would be fitting for a man who gave
his love to words, hear my humble plea,
as I, not denounced as you were denounced,
not affronted as you were affronted,
without your exile, shame or poverty,
cast my eyes back at labour without meaning,
words without substance, work without value,
and without knowing what I should take on:
that I may be wrong as you were wrong, that
this is not the end, but a turn in the road.

Translated by Niall O'Gallagher

XIII

nàmhaid a' sìor choiseachd aig do thaobh.
Leagadh do shaoghail fhèin gu làr, na bha
gaol agad air, na daoin', an ceàrn, an cànain,
b' e sin do bharail. Bha na sgrìobhadh leat
's na dh'obraich thu fàgte gun chèill, gun bhrìgh,
gun dùil ri leantainn air. Ach bha thu ceàrr!
'S e sin a dh'iarrainn èigheachd, mar gum b' ann
'nam sheasamh fhìn faisg ri do ghualainn-sa
a bhionn, am peann a spìonadh bho do làimh,
is dèanamh soilleir nach robh 'n obair agad

XIV

crìochnaicht', ach dìreach a' tòiseachadh,
nach ann air oir a shònraicheadh dhut àite
ach anns a' bhuillsgean fhèin, agus do chlaonadh,
mar a theireadh tu, gun bhith 'na bhacadh
ach 'na adhbhar leasachaidh aig t' obair.
Ged a chluinneas tu mi 'n-dràsta, 's dòcha,
chan fhaod mo ghuth siubhal cho fad' air ais
's gun ruig e thu am meadhan briseadh-dùil.
Ach, ma tha thu mothachail do chagar
de gach seòrsa, air cho lag 's gum bitheadh,

XV

mar a bu fhreagarrach do dhuin' a thug
a ghaol do fhaclan, èisd ri m' agairt ìosal,
's mi gun mo chàineadh mar a bha thu càinte,
gun a bhith peanasaichte mar a bhà thu,
gun fhògarrachd, gun adhbhar nàir', gun bhochdainn,
ach faicinn air mo chùl gnìomhachd gun bhrìgh,
fhaclan gun shusbaint, obrachadh nach fhiach,
's gun fhios agam gu dè ghabhainn os làimh:
gum bithinn-s' ceàrr mar a bha thusa ceàrr,
's nach ceann mo thurais seo, ach car san rathad.

Sheena Williamson

THE CHRONICLE OF HERON

Heron winches up into nimble, dabbled wafts
throughout this, his last tour of heavenly Archaeopteryx.
Jilted by Jurassic trees, he no longer trusts them
with his secret circus, high fixed feet.
River languishes infatuated with his light, beautiful scrolls,
trails after heron's each unwoven toe frond to untie them.
Slow ferried ghost fish drift in gauze gowns.
They fling jewels, bleed pearls and dive low
in silt disguises.
Unlike them heron was only just yesterday fish.
Still can't remember how it all happened.
Bright, his citrine eye, its glint of metal mixed
with sour Dominican, tin potash, as fire moulders
to sandy grit.
Filing smooth the tipped nap of his flint,
dipped hot in the cool ford, heron extinguishes his beak
even as it forms, holding rolling minnows wreathed in fire.
Only trees dripping wet from drowning the sun
under their plush plaids in North Inch Park's drenched winds
have been here long enough
to remember what heron-fish seemed to forget.

When the river first underwent
its gaze-rushed Garden of Eden intelligence test –
the one for guessing meddled ceramics
and arrangements for shattering bones –
heron immediately learned how to support his own weight
by wearing wings and there he was, everywhere home,
opening like a zip umbrella, lightning bolt
smitten with the limb of a biting tree.
Freeing leafy budded wrists
from his all-powerful yesterday fish-fins, he screamed
only to find himself 'Become First Bird'.

Never not looking better than gloriously towel-dried,
perturbed in the foliage of his matrimonial plumes
he stood and he stood till fish found him set

and by the time blowy winds finished feathering heron-fish
with epileptic snare-whelters he had become cross-dressed,
freak-frocked, effete. Always obvious if he moved,
nothing could be done save model himself to look
like all the other creatures or peer only at his beak.
In the water he could just see himself,
the colour of sky-suffered henge stone,
frozen under thunder's pewters.

But his heart beats warm in its blue basket of twigs,
lifting him as he gives, demure-disintegrating
into flight and now this bird is cast
sifting cremation ash from his own canopic jar.
Fanning out to wizard height,
he follows a straight line gripping his worn staff,
reviving the river from its noonday swoon.

Heron will drop down
to bring all rocks to rest in water.
Water is his god-given silver plate.
He tilts a lonely dilating eye
to his thirty-piece dinner set of girlish river
polished with circles of hill hair.
It's all mixed up, his minnow-fare.
The whole of his river has become stained
from dirty cups of mud emulsion
that tractors have dumped.
It must be shifted until everything is clear of silt
not just for heron's dinner but to mend
the many mirrors of sky.
When Heaven's soft layers tear and seasons become
ominously drier heron will remember
where he has hidden his fish book of spindling spells.

Listening to elegant water chanting
he will arc his bedraggled voice and his voice
will take him accelerating up
to the canopy of preternatural creaks.

Flying over his gargoyle buttress above the bank
he will bring all sea to spate
and spare no person who does not look back
to recognize that it is he, heron-fish, who survived,
indeed preceded the weight of the first atomic impact.
That fiery asteroid still cooling in his prehistoric
iris.

Jim C. Wilson

WHAT'S LEFT

The glass
you drank from sits
amongst the napkins, crumbs.
I see the prints of your fingers
and lips.

THE NEXT POEM

Watch as the moon moves slowly over
the distant domes of Sacré-Coeur,
and the skin on your face is like linen.

Feel in your palm the cool bloodless hand
of the pale Madonna who lost her faith;
she parts her lips for you alone.

Then go to one of those rooms in Paris,
high in the prow of a shiplike building,
your view an unending boulevard.

Close the dust-hung velvet drapes;
listen for breathing that is not yours,
and wait there for hours or forever.

The world might mutate, while your tongue
strains hard to articulate. Pray that words
will tumble out, the Seine will fill with stars.

Matthew Wright

DANCE WITH ME

Dance with me,
Glam rocker,
Make me feel like I know
You know how
Pout, aim a wink at me;
Blow a kiss
This way. Sprinkle glitter
Dust onto my
brow, take
my tender
hand in
yours. Contort
my body;
Tell me
my hair
looks pretty.
Compliment my
70s boots and
their heels –
they are
like yours
you know!
Hold me
as you
would your
guitar, wear
me around
your neck.
Rock me; Strum me

To your own unique

Tune, play a riff

From my flesh, pluck
My chest strings perhaps.

Plant your lipstick on
My face, take me
now. Sing of
Our space, make it real!
All imperfections fall away.

Take me there in your
Tin can; take me
To the stars.

BIOGRAPHIES

Gregor Addison was born in 1966 in Dalkeith. He attended Newbattle Abbey College and Aberdeen University where he studied English and Gaelic. He has taught both over the past ten years and is now a lecturer at Clydebank College. He is currently working on two novels (*Phusis* and *Teufelsdrokh*) and lives in Scotstoun with his pet elk Elgar.

Following Scottish Screen's 2000 *MovieMakars* course, **Colin Begg** had screenplays shortlisted in several competitions and in 2004 wrote Australian short *Alice*. A Scottish Screen bursary helped his studies at UTS Sydney, including Martin Harrison's poetry workshops. Colin's poems featured in *LooseLips* and *Reportage*. His latest project is **www.peatpoets.com** with Craig Stobo.

Laura Bissell recently attained a first class degree in Theatre Studies and English Literature at Glasgow University, where she now tutors. Laura spent eighteen months in Australia studying theatre, literature and performance and intends to continue her studies there at postgraduate level, researching contemporary theatre practice, while continuing writing short plays and poems and devising performance.

Norman Bissell is an EIS Area Officer who lives in Glasgow, directs the Scottish Centre for Geopoetics and Alba Editions, and writes poems, essays and book reviews which have appeared in magazines, books and newspapers. These Luing poems are from his forthcoming collection *Earth, Sea and Sky*.

Jim Carruth was born in Johnstone in 1963 and has spent most of his adult life in Renfrewshire. A widely published poet, his first collection, *Bovine Pastoral*, published in 2004 by Ludovic Press, was runner-up in the Callum Macdonald Memorial Award. A new collection, *High Auchensale*, is due in autumn 2006.

Ian Crockatt has a particular interest in writing series of poems and 'Viking Spring' opens his latest, *Skald*. Its form is derived from the intricate syllabic rhyming and alliterative verse of Viking poets, or Skalds, of the 9th to 13th centuries. It's best read out loud.

Tracey Emerson lives in Edinburgh. She started writing fiction in 2003 and was a runner-up in the 2004 Scotsman and Orange Short Story Award. She recently received a New Writer's bursary from the Scottish Arts Council and is writing more short stories as well as starting her first novel.

Hazel Frew was born in 1968 and grew up in Broughty Ferry, Dundee. She graduated from Glasgow University in 1991 with Honours in Sociology. From 1996 she has been published in *The Rialto*, *Pulsar*, *Cutting Teeth*, *Nerve*, *Poetry Scotland* and *Air*. Her poems have been accepted for publication in 2006 by *Orbis* and *Painted, spoken*. She also writes short stories and articles.

William Gilfedder was born and raised in Glasgow. And left school at 15. And has lived and worked in the city all his life. And has had a variety of jobs in and around the city. He has published poems in various magazines including *The Scottish Review*, *Mungo's Tongues* edited by Hamish Whyte, and eight previous issues of *New Writing Scotland*.

Paul Gorman, 31, is married and lives in Midlothian. Shortlisted for the 2002 Dundee Book Prize, his work has appeared in several Scottish literary magazines, including *New Writing Scotland 23*.

Rody Gorman was born in Dublin in 1960 and now lives on the Isle of Skye. He has published numerous poetry collections in English, Irish and Scottish Gaelic. His selected poems, *Chernilo*, are published by Coiscéim in 2006. He is the editor and co-publisher of the Irish and Scottish Gaelic poetry anthology *An Guth*, and is Convener of the Translation and Linguistic Rights Committee of Scottish PEN.

Charlie Gracie is originally from Baillieston – land of poets. He now lives in Thornhill near Stirling with his family. He has had poetry and short stories published in a number of places in recent years including *Cutting Teeth*, *Pushing Out* *the Boat*, *Poetry Scotland*, *New Writing Scotland* (*19*, *20*, *21* and *23*) and the *Herald* 'poem of the day'. In his work he tries to capture what glimmers or lurks just beyond the surface.

Lis Lee, a former journalist, lives and writes in Kelso in the Scottish Borders following her move from the Isle of Mull. This is her third appearance in *New Writing Scotland*. An SAC bursary in 2004 enabled her to complete a first collection, *Sob Sister*, in 2005.

Joanna Lilley first saw inukshuks back in 1991 when she cycled nearly 6,000 miles from one corner of Canada to the other, ending up in Inuvik in the Northwest Territories, the end of the road. She's had a thing about them ever since. Joanna writes poems, short stories and novels.

Andrew McCallum hails from Biggar, a small town in South Lanarkshire that aspires to Borderiety. He is the current Secretary of Biggar Museum Trust's Brownsbank Committee, which maintains Hugh MacDiarmid's last home as a national resource and supports local writing in the community through the Brownsbank Fellowship writer-in-residency scheme.

Stuart Robert Macdonald was born and brought up in south-west Scotland. He currently lives in Edinburgh with his wife and children where he works as a data librarian. He's been published widely in numerous magazines and anthologies. He is still working on a first collection.

Frank McHugh is an Irish Scotsman, living in Ayrshire, who devotes his life to music, language and his children. He can trace his love of poetry back to Jim Carroll's classes on Hopkins. In previous incarnations he was a musician and lived in Euskadi. He presently earns a crust teaching.

Martin MacIntyre was born in 1965, brought up in Lenzie, Glasgow, and attended St Aloysius' College, Aberdeen University and Sabhal Mòr Ostaig. Publications include *Ath-Aithne* (*Reacquaintance*), a collection of short stories which won the Saltire Society First Book Award 2003, and

Gymnippers Dicidian (*Wednesday Gymnippers*), an urban-based novel, shortlisted for the Saltire Society Book of the Year 2005. His first collection of poetry will be published later in 2006 by Luath Press. Martin now lives in Edinburgh with his wife and two children.

David S. Mackenzie is from Easter Ross and lives in London. He is the author of one novel, *The Truth of Stone* (Mainstream). Look out for *The Interpretations*.

Jane Irina McKie has been living in Scotland for the past five years – first Edinburgh, and latterly Glasgow. Last year she received a New Writers' bursary from the Scottish Arts Council, and her first full collection of poems, *Morocco Rococo*, is coming out in early 2007 with Cinnamon Press.

Iain S. MacPherson is from Canada originally. Apart from poetry in Gaelic, French and English, and lecturing at Sabhal Mòr Ostaig-UHI, he is a freelance Middle-East analyst for BBC Radio nan Gaidheal. He is also writing a screenplay for a feature-length Gaelic *Dogme* film, 'Indian Summer', with *Young Films* and *Scottish Screen*.

Lyn Moir's *Me and Galileo* (2001) and *Breakers' Yard* (2003) are published by Arrowhead Press. She is currently working on a collection based on Velázquez's *Las Meninas* and Picasso's versions of it. She lives in St Andrews.

Jacklin Murray was born in Fort William and brought up on Mull. A civil servant for twenty years, now working for Capability Scotland. Married to Pat, a restaurant manager. He has been with Erskine Writers for four years and has won competitions including Radio Scotland's Cover Stories (2004) Christmas competition.

Ronnie Nixon ran a picture-framing business and gallery in the West End of Glasgow for a number of years. He then returned to teaching art in a secondary school, taking early retirement a few years ago.

Niall O'Gallagher is a writer and musician. He stays in Glasgow.

Vix Parker is 29 and lives in the Highlands with her cat, Maisy. She has had stories published in *The Eildon Tree* and *Random Acts of Writing*, and is working up to a novel.

Mary Paulson-Ellis is currently working on a novel from which this piece is taken. She has a fourteen-year-old son and lives in Edinburgh with her partner. This is the first time she has been properly published.

Julia Rampen is 16 and lives in Edinburgh. She was introduced to writing poetry last year, as part of her Standard Grade English, but she has always enjoyed writing in general. Her other interests include music and art, and Woodcraft Folk, a youth organisation.

After many years at the chalk face, **June Ritchie** is trying to write. She has written children's plays, silly verse, poetry and prose. She has had poetry published in anthologies and a story included in *A Sense of Place* 2005.

Alison Swinfen was born and brought up in Sheffield, did a degree in French and German at the University of Durham and a PhD at the University of Sheffield. She lives and works in Glasgow and is a member of the Iona Community.

Judith Taylor comes from Coupar Angus (somebody has to) and now lives and works in Aberdeen, where she is a member of Lemon Tree Writers. Her poetry has been published in a number of magazines in Scotland and the UK.

Born and raised in Malaysia, **Chiew Siah Tei** is currently completing a PhD in Creative Writing at Glasgow University while working on her first novel. She scripted *Night Swimmer* which won Best Short Film at Vendome in 2000. Her play *Three Thousand Troubled Threads* was staged at the Edinburgh International Festival 2005.

Fiona Ritchie Walker is originally from Montrose, Angus, and now lives in Blaydon, near Newcastle. She has two poetry collections: *Lip Reading* (Diamond Twig) and *Garibaldi's Legs* (Iron Press). A chapbook, *Angus Palette* (Sand), with illustrations by her sister, Kirsten Ritchie Walker, will be published in 2006. **www.fionaritchiewalker.co.uk**

Jane Webster is a middle-aged Scotswoman with weaknesses for wearing stilettos and writing short stories. She loves herons, red kites and her work as a mental-health practitioner. Her greatest claim to literary fame to date is being runner-up in the *Racing Post* short-story competition.

Christopher Whyte is a prize-winning poet in Gaelic and the author of four novels in English. He worked in Italy from 1973 to 1985, taught at Glasgow University from 1990 to 2005, and now lives in Budapest, Hungary. He has translated three of Pasolini's 'poemi' into English.

Sheena Williamson rarely publishes. She rescues birds, takes comfort from remarkable stones, water and God. Her poems are written by ghosts.

Jim C. Wilson lives in East Lothian. He has been widely published for over twenty years, and has won the Scottish International Open Poetry Competition twice. He has been a Royal Literary Fund Fellow since 2001, and has run Poetry in Practice sessions at Edinburgh University since 1994.

Matthew Wright discovered a passion for poetry at university. It was relevant to his degree but became a hobby, with topics ranging from the surrounding world to human relationships. He now focuses his writing on the one thing that truly matters to him – his relationship with Jesus.